GREETINGS FROM
AFGHANISTAN
SEND MORE AMMO

Facing page: Captain Benjamin Tupper and his ETT partner, Corporal Radoslaw "Ski" Polanski.

GREETINGS FROM
AFGHANISTAN
SEND MORE AMMO

DISPATCHES
FROM TALIBAN
COUNTRY

Benjamin Tupper

NAL
CALIBER

NAL CALIBER
Published by New American Library, a division of
Penguin Group (USA) Inc., 375 Hudson Street,
New York, New York 10014, USA
Penguin Group (Canada), 90 Eglinton Avenue East, Suite 700, Toronto,
Ontario M4P 2Y3, Canada (a division of Pearson Penguin Canada Inc.)
Penguin Books Ltd., 80 Strand, London WC2R 0RL, England
Penguin Ireland, 25 St. Stephen's Green, Dublin 2,
Ireland (a division of Penguin Books Ltd.)
Penguin Group (Australia), 250 Camberwell Road, Camberwell, Victoria 3124,
Australia (a division of Pearson Australia Group Pty. Ltd.)
Penguin Books India Pvt. Ltd., 11 Community Centre, Panchsheel Park,
New Delhi - 110 017, India
Penguin Group (NZ), 67 Apollo Drive, Rosedale, North Shore 0632,
New Zealand (a division of Pearson New Zealand Ltd.)
Penguin Books (South Africa) (Pty.) Ltd., 24 Sturdee Avenue,
Rosebank, Johannesburg 2196, South Africa

Penguin Books Ltd., Registered Offices:
80 Strand, London WC2R 0RL, England

First published by NAL Caliber, an imprint of New American Library,
a division of Penguin Group (USA) Inc.

First Printing, June 2010
10   9   8   7   6   5   4   3   2   1

LIBRARY OF CONGRESS CATALOGING-IN-PUBLICATION DATA:
Tupper, Benjamin, 1969–
Greetings from Afghanistan, send more ammo: dispatches from Taliban country/
Benjamin Tupper.
p. cm.
ISBN 978-0-451-23143-7
1. Afghan War, 2001—Personal narratives, American.   2. Counterinsurgency—Afghanistan—
History—21st century.   3. Insurgency—Afghanistan—History—21st century.   4. Taliban.
5. Tupper, Benjamin, 1969–   6. Soldiers—United States—Biography.   7. United States. National
Guard Bureau—Biography.   8. Afghan War, 2001—Social aspects.   9. Afghanistan—Social
conditions—21st century.   10. Afghanistan—Social life and customs—21st century. I. Title.
DS371.413.T87.2010
958.104'7—dc22   2010003843

Set in Visage
Designed by Patrice Sheridan

Printed in the United States of America

PUBLISHER'S NOTE
Penguin is committed to publishing works of quality and integrity. In that spirit, we are proud
to offer this book to our readers; however the story, the experiences and the words are the
author's alone.
While the author has made every effort to provide accurate telephone numbers and Internet
addresses at the time of publication, neither the publisher nor the author assumes any
responsibility for errors, or for changes that occur after publication. Further, publisher does not
have any control over and does not assume any responsibility for author or third-party Web
sites or their content.

To the Afghan soldiers, the combat interpreters,

and the War Eagle and Blackfoot ETTs:

_____

Your courage and bravery kept me alive.

Your humility and willingness to sacrifice for the greater

good of the mission inspired me.

Your example of transcending differences in culture,

language, and religion assured me that the foundation for a

new, tolerant, and peaceful Afghanistan will be built upon

your legacy.

_____

CONTENTS

The three musicians sat with legs crossed on the floor around me, sipping *chai* as our interpreter translated their stories for the handful of Americans present. The musicians spoke softly, in a calm tone that suggested an uneventful and ordinary story. Perhaps for Afghans living through the reign of the Taliban, these were normal stories: imprisonment and torture for playing their music, threats against family members, and burying instruments to prevent the Taliban from confiscating and destroying them.

Earlier in the day, I had visited the Afghan National Museum in Kabul, where I was greeted by defaced statues, shattered pottery, and torn canvases. This home to Afghan art history had borne the brunt of the Taliban's war on culture. In a corner of the museum sat the masterpiece of their destructive work: a large display case housing hundreds of paintings and drawings that spanned generations of artists. The paintings were all ripped into pieces by zealous Taliban foot soldiers.

It was on this day that I decided I wanted to play a part

in this war. I was in Afghanistan as a civilian with an NGO called Afghans4Tomorrow, but the sense of outrage that I felt witnessing firsthand what the Taliban had done was so profound, I needed to be more involved fighting them. Two years later, I would return to Afghanistan as a soldier. My decision to come back had nothing to do with the flag-waving politics that had swept America. It had nothing to do with September 11. Instead, I felt Americans had a moral and historical obligation to help stabilize Afghanistan, after we had abruptly disengaged from the country at the conclusion of the Afghan-Russian war. Our disappearing act in 1990 led directly to a decade of civil war, and ultimately to the Taliban taking over most of the country. For years the world sat by while the Taliban enslaved women and purged art and culture from Afghanistan. Now I had a chance, in my own small way, to work to undo this error, and to ensure that the next generation of Afghan girls could attend school, and that artists could paint, and musicians sing, without fear of torture and imprisonment.

GREETINGS FROM
AFGHANISTAN
SEND MORE AMMO

INTRODUCTION

ETTS: THE TIP OF THE COUNTERINSURGENCY SPEAR

orget what you know about the American Army. Strip from your mind the familiar images of U.S. soldiers fighting their way through Germany, Korea, or Vietnam. The essays you are about to read reveal another side of the American soldier's experience at war: individual soldiers removed from the comfort and familiarity of their Army units and placed into the ramshackle, newly formed Afghan National Army.

These American soldiers are the ETTs, the Embedded Training Teams. An average ETT team consists of sixteen American soldiers, embedded into an Afghan battalion of about five hundred soldiers. These ETTs are separated into teams of two, each team assigned to its own individual Afghan National Army company of about one hundred Afghan soldiers. They are embedded into these foreign ranks with little knowledge of Afghanistan's language, history, or culture, and they are forced, often in the heat of battle, to abandon the American doctrine of warfare and embrace creativity, patience, and primitive war-fighting techniques.

These essays are my personal stories as a member of this force in Afghanistan. ETTs are Marines, Army, and most often Army National Guard officers and NCOs assigned to the fledgling Afghan National Army (ANA), where they are tasked with the daunting mission of training the ANA in garrison, leading it in combat, and mentoring it to a final victory against a thriving and brutal Taliban insurgency.

These essays provide an introduction to the Afghan war as seen through the partnership of the ANA and the ETTs, forming the literal "tip of the spear" in the counterinsurgency fight. They chronicle the personal experiences of two ETTs: myself, Captain Benjamin Tupper (Infantry), and my partner, Corporal Radoslaw Polanski, also an infantryman. The stories vary in their scope, from personal war stories of our successes and failures in combat, to observations of day-to-day life inside the Afghan Army; the humorous moments, the culture clashes, the voice-raising arguments, and the differing roles that religion, women, and politics play in the lives of Afghans and the American soldiers assigned to train them.

This collection of essays also explores the injuries inflicted during war, from the slow but steady degradation of healthy minds by combat stress, to treating the physical wounds of combat, to the deaths of our comrades and enemies.

To understand Afghanistan's culture, its potential for modernization and democracy, and its remaining military challenges, one must walk in the shoes of the Afghan people and its Army. From May 2006 to May 2007, I walked in those shoes. These essays are the footprints of my journey.

Members of the 3rd Company, 2nd Battalion, 1st Brigade, 203rd Corps of the Afghan National Army, along with Captain Tupper (center, rear).

SECTION 1

WAR STORIES

EMBRACE THE SUCK

I first heard the phrase *embrace the suck* in Pittsburgh in 2001. I was in the living room of a college buddy, nursing a hangover, and flipping through a popular national magazine. Inside was an unsanitized article about field conditions in America's newest war: Afghanistan. The list of hardships that soldiers were experiencing in the heat and dust was described in vivid detail. But the spirits of the American infantrymen were undeterred. Their Zen-like approach was to "embrace the suck," a strategy of treating the hardships as friends, not enemies, and driving on.

Less than two weeks after my arrival in Ghazni, I was baptized by sweat and filth into this brotherhood of suffering and misery. I had just returned from a weeklong mission in the field with our ANA infantry battalion when I found myself in awe over the degradation of my physical body in such a short time.

Operation Desert Lion, as it was called, consisted of a series of sweeps deep into remote corners of Ghazni Province, with overnight bivouacs in various district centers. The

Suck Meter patches, commonly worn by ETTs and Special Forces soldiers. These unauthorized patches were a comical reference to the need to "embrace the suck."

operation, my first personal foray into real-world warfare, ended up being quite successful. We captured over a dozen suspected Taliban foot soldiers, and the Afghan National Police (ANP) captured a confirmed al-Qaeda regional commander. No friendly forces were killed or injured.

But death and injury are only two of the three facets of physical harm that confront a soldier. After this operation, we all suffered from the third facet of physical harm: the generalized internal and external human deterioration that occurs on long combat missions. This source of misery is perhaps best described simply as "the suck": the dozens of small, needling things that torment and plague the body when it is deprived of sanitation, sleep, and proper nourishment. A quick exploration of the major manifestations is worthwhile, and serves as a good backdrop for understanding how one feels while out on missions. When reading the accounts of soldiers, it's a good idea to keep these persistent physical problems in mind. They are constant companions in our lives at war, and should be dampers to whatever excitement the reader may feel about the thrill and appeal of combat.

Nourishment: I'm not sure whether it's the heat or the stress or the quality of food, but your body shuts off its natural hunger drive once you enter this high-stress environment. Within the first three weeks at Ghazni, I lost fourteen pounds. The food tasted bland. Thinking about good meals back home made me nauseous. Eventually, you eat simply because you will pass out if you don't. There are times when you are running and gunning, and you can't even remember the last time you ate. Yet you have no sense of being hungry.

Heat: It's hot in Ghazni, over one hundred degrees in the noonday summer sun. When you think of hot weather, you think of shorts, T-shirts, air-conditioning, and a nice fan. The reality here is the opposite. Once you put on the full coat of combat attire, you resemble someone properly suited for winter climates, not extreme heat.

At all times, despite this brutal dry heat, we wear a helmet, the long-sleeve and long-pants Army Combat Uniform (ACU, the digitalized camouflage uniform), gloves, and the coup de grâce—fifty pounds of body armor. The body armor is the most egregious when it comes to ventilation. Within minutes, your complete torso is soaked through with sweat, and it remains that way all day. The only time you dry out is when the mission is over and it's safe to take off the body armor. Add to this outfit heavy boots, thick socks, elbow and knee pads, and voilà, you've got a 100 percent effective heat-retaining and heat-maximizing uniform.

Granted, there is a practical reason for all the protective equipment and gear. Our body armor can take rifle shots point-blank and keep us bruised but alive. The complete coverage of the uniform's pattern effectively allows you to blend into the environment, making target identification of your form harder for the enemy. In the end, the irony is that the ensemble of gear that keeps us alive is the same one that makes us wish we were dead so we can escape the heat and discomfort it produces.

Sleep: When we are out on overnight missions, sleep becomes an impediment to getting the job done, and it's treated that way. There is very little in the way of a sleep pattern during combat operations, so your body is constantly groggy as its circadian rhythm is being destroyed.

Nighttime is also the most dangerous time for a soldier, so sleep is never deep, nor is it refreshing. The nights are disrupted by the shifts one must take pulling security, and the sleeping conditions are austere at best. During Operation Desert Lion, we bivouacked inside a dilapidated and abandoned mud-walled compound. Scattered among our sleeping bags was trash, dried human feces, the remains of dead dogs, and the refuse from battles long gone by—bullet casings and RPG-7 rocket ballast tubes.

Some of us slept on the dirty ground, others moved away from the detritus, up to the mud roof of the sole structure inside the compound. This provided a good place to set up our machine gun in case the Taliban decided to pay us a late-night visit. During Desert Lion, the War Eagle ETTs got about three hours of sleep a night, after running twenty-hour high-tempo operations during the day.

Hygiene: Any idea of keeping clean in the heat and filth of this combat environment is just fantasy. The cleanest body is defiled with dirt and sweat within thirty minutes of the onset of activity. The dust covers every pore, but the inside of your nose and sinuses get the worst of it. These areas are simultaneously being dried by the arid hot air and bathed in fine dust particles. Within hours, the nose becomes a factory for bloody, sticky slugs of brown snot. The more you blow your nose, the more it bleeds, so you learn to just let the slugs cohabitate in your sinuses.

The rest of your body doesn't fare much better. Your skin, hands, face, and hair all get greasy and dirty, which you just have to accept. Acne hits you like a thirteen-year-old in puberty. I've already talked about the sweat from the uniform; suffice to say that your body stinks and itches and just plain feels nasty. Having all this filth on you is an invitation to all sorts of internal and external friends—fungus, bacteria, and parasites. On the outside, you get to itching in places only your doctor and your lover have ever laid eyes on.

In my case, the most interesting area of desecration was my feet. I literally had to peel off my socks when we returned from one long mission, because they had crusted onto, and become part of, my skin. While removing them, I had to fight off nausea from the smell of rotting flesh and Limburger cheese. My feet had tiny red dots on them, skin peeling off in moist white patties, and yellow, greasy blobs all over. I think the yellow blobs were the source of the horrific smell. It may seem silly, but many times when the action is finally done for the day, and you can at last lie down, the last thing you worry about is getting clean. The weight of physical and mental exhaustion trumps hunger and hygiene every time.

What goes on inside the body is equally disturbing. You

fluctuate between trying to crap cinder blocks and having the power squirts. That nice, predictable dump you took back home is a distant memory. Oh, and to add insult to injury, there are no toilets anywhere, and it's a war, so you've got to stay with your soldiers for self-protection and security. There is no privacy during these nice downloads.

I could go on and on, but I'm sure you get the picture. The day-to-day effects on your body suck, and if you don't embrace it and roll with it, it will destroy any morale and motivation you have to accomplish your mission. So, as infantry soldiers have done for millennia, we make humor out of our problems and try to keep them from making us so sick that we can't do our jobs.

ETTS: THE TALIBAN'S HIGH-VALUE TARGET

One could make a reasonable and rational argument that being an ETT in a frontline ANA infantry *kandak* (the Afghan word for battalion) is the most dangerous job in Afghanistan. While traditional American units engage the enemy in Afghanistan with the best weapons, logistics, and communication, the ETT member often finds himself without support in any of these areas. Most American soldiers would scoff at the suggestion they go outside the wire with only one fellow soldier, in one vehicle with one medium machine gun. Under today's rules of engagement in Afghanistan, American combat commanders at any level would reject any such mission to their forces as an unacceptable risk. Yet this risk was the daily fare for myself and many of my fellow ETTs in Afghanistan in 2006 and 2007. With my partner, Corporal Radek Polanski, a.k.a. Ski, and our weathered up-armored Humvee and our M240 Bravo machine gun, we would seek and pursue the enemy, accompanied only by our unpredictable hodgepodge of Afghan soldiers and their unarmored Ford Ranger pickups. Once we left the wire of our ANA Forward Operating Base, we were on our own while out on our mission.

Ski and I operated without the broad range of services provided to U.S. units on similar missions. For example, we traversed mined roads with no U.S. engineer route-clearing package support, something U.S. maneuver units regularly could rely on to clear their roads in advance of such missions. We treated our ANA wounded knowing we were unlikely candidates for medevac, and we were low on the list for close air support (CAS). We were never the main effort, so in the rare case we got CAS, it was hours late or ill-suited for the task at hand.

The isolation and limited support of the ETTs was not lost on the enemy. The Taliban insurgency, despite their

Ghazni Province: War Eagle ETT Humvee after IED hit. ANA vehicles had passed over the device previously, but it was detonated under the ETT Humvee.

dirty clothes and rusted weapons, are a bold, creative, and thriving movement that spends more time studying our habits and tactics than fighting us. The result is that when they hit, they have a high rate of success. My experience was that we rarely found them and they always found us. And when they found us, it wasn't a pleasant encounter.

The ETTs, with their sole Humvee, were easily identified by the Taliban and were the focal point of enemy fire. Even though the Afghan soldiers accompanying us provided less armored and more numerous targets, the ETTs were understood to be the nerve center of the operation. The Taliban were well aware of our Humvee's communications capabilities, and we were targeted accordingly. Additionally, when Afghan soldiers were wounded or killed, or their leaders faltered, the ETTs didn't bug out. But when an ETT was hit, the psychological effect on the ANA could be paralyzing.

THE FLIP-FLOP ARMY

The Afghan National Army is a work in progress. It has lots of potential, but it also has great deficits that it must overcome in order to establish itself as a credible national security force. As I see it, the ANA has two primary missions: defeating domestic enemies and protecting against international adversaries. Both goals are currently unreachable and unrealistic without continued U.S. and Coalition support. The ETT mission was created to help speed the ANA's development along, but I'm finding that despite our best efforts, old habits and deficiencies die hard.

First, I'll start with the good news. The average ANA grunt is as brave as, if not braver than, your average American soldier, or any nation's soldiers, for that matter. The aggressive pursuit of the enemy, even at great personal danger, is a trait found among many in the ANA. At the first shots fired, the ANA are like hunting dogs anxious for the chase. Sometimes they break and lose their combat effectiveness, but on the whole they are more likely to aggressively react to enemy contact than not.

The second positive aspect of the ANA is that, despite low pay, poor living conditions, and chronic lack of supplies, the morale of the ANA is high. ANA soldiers regularly go out on missions without enough food, ammo, or water, yet do so without hesitation and still succeed. When it's fighting time, all the shortages and problems cease to be an issue.

Another positive aspect is that the problems in Iraq with enemy infiltration and manipulation of the armed forces are not as serious here. It would be naive to say there are no enemy infiltrators in the ANA's ranks, but their number and influence is barely measurable. Perhaps the best proof of this is the fact that I have never, in the dozens of missions out with the ANA, hesitated to turn my back on any ANA soldier. I trust them with my life daily, and to date, it's been kept in good hands.

Last, I have never ceased to be amazed at how well the ANA soldiers understand their role as low-level representatives of the Government of Afghanistan. They go out of their way to talk to civilians about building a new country, free from the violence and corruption and the warlordism of the past. These soldiers form an army that is a melting pot of tribes, languages, and sects, and they perform as a team time and time again. Their example to the civilians they interact with must leave an impression that gives hope for the future.

But it's not all peaches and cream. The Afghan Army, despite these positive attributes, has serious problems. The chronic shortages previously mentioned are in part due to corruption at higher levels. Senior officers, NCOs, and common soldiers have stolen, pilfered, and sold Army property, and do so at times with impunity. Even at the lowest levels, underpaid soldiers frequently take newly issued items to the bazaar to sell. When you ask them the next day where these items are, they will insist they were never issued to them. While wrong, theft at this level is more understandable because the soldiers barely make enough to feed a family.

One story comes to mind to highlight this specific problem. While out on a mission, and in hot pursuit of the enemy, my Humvee hit a series of irrigation canals that caused the spare tire and a fuel can to go flying off the vehicle's rear cargo cage. Given the urgency of the moment, they were left abandoned for later pickup (or so I thought). Upon arrival at our destination, we were informed by the ANA that they had picked up our items for us and were safely storing them in the back of one of their pickup trucks.

Upon completion of the mission we returned to the Forward Operating Base (FOB), but it was dark and we were all tired, so I made the (incorrect) decision to collect the items in the morning. The next day, I scoured the ANA FOB for my tire and fuel can, but found neither. No one knew where they were, but everyone I talked to was happy to send me on a wild-goose chase following up false leads. Finally, and quite by accident, I came across a well-concealed but slightly visible Humvee tire, which I returned to the vehicle. However, the fuel can and its contents joined the permanent ranks of the "missing in action."

As for the ANA being a "flip-flop Army," it is not for the reason you may assume. The ANA does not flip-flop its loyalties. From top to bottom, it's firmly committed to fighting and destroying al-Qaeda and the Taliban. No, the flip-flop refers to footwear. Yes, that's right: the cheap plastic sandals that are a beachgoing standard in the States.

The flip-flop is the preferred choice of the ANA for daily soldier life. Sure, they have boots, but flip-flops are so much more comfortable in formation, or even when meeting with your commander. And if flip-flops are out of season, basketball sneakers will do just fine. Comfort apparently trumps uniformity (something the U.S. military should consider!).

Personal modification of the standard uniform does not stop at ground level. Head wear is equally versatile. Hunter green berets, the officially issued uniform headgear, are usually replaced with do-rags, Arab-style head scarves, and baseball caps. And to finish off the customizing of the uniform, throw on a pair of tinted swimming Speedo goggles (as one of our soldiers does), and you've got a ready-to-rock-and-roll ANA soldier. Some of these guys look like they just came off the set of *The Road Warrior.* I keep waiting for Mad Max to roll up and tell us where the fuel truck is located.

Perhaps the most intriguing and puzzling habit of many ANA soldiers is their use of henna. I commonly walk through

ANA soldiers in flip-flops, despite subzero temperatures.

In the spirit of fairness and full disclosure, it should be pointed out that many ETTs also modify their uniforms, favoring the use of unauthorized homemade patches (mine are pictured above), baseball caps, and nonregulation hiking boots in place of combat boots.

Third Company's barracks in the morning to find a large number of soldiers with hands painted orange with flowers and other assorted designs. Some have orange hair. Others are busy painting their fingernails with henna, reminding me of thirteen-year-old girls at a slumber party. I just shake my head, pass around greetings, and move on. When they start putting on the lipstick, then I'll get worried.

DONKEYS AND GRENADES: FIRST COMBAT

My first combat engagement was nothing like I expected. The action was anticlimactic, the anticipated gunfire and explosions were minimal, and the greatest threat I faced was from friendly forces.

The operation was unplanned. It originated as a 911 emergency mission, the kind that arrived via radio, cell phone, or a speeding Afghan National Police truck screeching onto our FOB. The scenario was always the same: overwhelming Taliban forces running rampant in this village or that mountain range. When we get the word there are Taliban in a known location, our ANA battalion spins up a company-sized element, the ETT commander adds a Humvee to the mix, and we all go hunting.

On this day, the Provincial Reconstruction Team Ghazni (known as PRT Ghazni) also put together a quick reaction force, or QRF, which maneuvered onto the alleged enemy position from a different axis of advance. In Ghazni, the PRT was a U.S. FOB located five kilometers south of our ANA FOB.

As our ANA element drove south through small villages of Andar district, we engaged in sporadic running gunfights with a handful of motorcycle-mounted Taliban. Motorcycles are the preferred method of maneuver for the Taliban in the Ghazni area, and they can outrun our Humvees and ANA pickup trucks with ease.

Each time we stopped to exchange shots, the Taliban were on the move before we could dismount and get a bead on them. I heard my War Eagle ETT teammates Vandy and Deghand cussing on the radio about almost having the Taliban in their sites, only to be foiled by a last-second motorcycle escape.

After half an hour of "shoot and scoot," the Taliban decided to change tactics and ditched their motorcycles and weapons and pretended to be civilians. We captured two Taliban in a well pump house, wiping grease on their faces, trying to look like authentic well-house workers. We also picked up a local mullah, who had been agitating people to fight the "infidels" (meaning us). After he had been detained, he made a point of telling our interpreters that he would like to have the opportunity to slit my throat.

Eventually, our ANA element linked up with the PRT Ghazni forces from the Connecticut National Guard's Bravo Company, 102nd Infantry Battalion, 29th Division. The arrival of Bravo Company's soldiers was delayed by a forced detour. While driving toward our position, their lead Humvee was spared destruction by the poor timing of a donkey. As the vehicle drove into a small village, the donkey walked into the road in front of the Humvee and stepped on a pressure-plate antitank mine. The resulting explosion was both catastrophic and fortunate. It was catastrophic for the donkey, which ended up in large pieces scattered throughout the village. For the soldiers, the results were more favorable, as they lived to tell the tale. The convoy of Bravo Company vehicles did an about-face and chose another route, which made sense, as mines usually are emplaced in small groups.

After the enemy had either been captured or had escaped, the ETTs, ANA, and Bravo Company soldiers compared notes on the day's events. Then word came of a follow-on emergency mission from the ANP. They reported being surrounded by Taliban, so our ETT Humvee and our ANA mounted up and moved to assist them. By the time we got to their position, a mud-walled compound, the Taliban had long since left, and the surrounded ANP were nowhere to be found. What we did find, though, was an unexploded grenade, tossed by the Taliban into the compound. It had fortunately failed to detonate, and the family that lived within hoped the ANA would dispose of it.

In the American Army, an Explosive Ordnance Disposal (EOD) unit might be called to take care of this problem. But in the ANA, the solution is a little more informal. Within minutes, two ANA soldiers had been selected to get rid of the unexploded grenade—by shooting it.

The initial shots were successful only in traumatizing the poor farm animals living inside the compound. They bucked and ran around like the sky was falling. When the two selected soldiers proved less than accurate, a new group was selected, and began firing their AK-47s with single well-aimed shots.

And here in this compound, surrounded by friendly forces and frightened livestock, with the sun casually setting over the horizon, I was almost killed.

Perhaps it was my rookie status, or just my innocent curiosity at witnessing my first Afghan EOD project, but I definitely failed to grasp the potential danger of the situation, in part because the ANA soldiers were so nonchalant about it. Corporal Polanski, who had arrived in country three months before me, recognized the lethal folly taking place and retreated back to his position in the Humvee. Other ETTs fell back to a safer distance. I, however, remained standing in the doorway to the compound, most likely with a dumb grin on my face.

When the grenade exploded, the already traumatized livestock shuddered. The cow listed sideways, the goats jumped, and some just collapsed in place. All these reactions were more out of shock and terror than actual injury.

The explosion echoed off the thick interior walls of the compound, as did the grenade fragmentation, which kicked up little clouds of dirt as it ricocheted around me and into the mud walls and dirt floors. Through some stroke of luck, no living creature, be it two-legged or four-legged, was injured in this unwise endeavor.

The Taliban-supporting mullah who wanted to slit my throat.

26 JUNE: SURROUNDED

After eight peaceful days of no missions and easy living, we finally got tasked with a presence patrol to a group of neighboring villages in Andar district, our "hottest" area vis-à-vis enemy activity.

At our first stop, all was well. One of the first signs of trouble is a lack of people out in the village, especially children. If children come out to see you, you might as well put away your rifle, because it means the enemy is not around. In this case, a lot of kids came out to see us on our first stop, so we relaxed and passed out pens and candy, and made small talk with the boys who were interested in chatting.

Eventually, we met with some village elders, who confirmed that there were Taliban operating in the area but said they only saw a few now and then. Everything seemed fine, and after an hour of friendly small talk we bid them farewell and mounted up for our second stop, a neighboring village less than a mile away.

En route to the next village, we were immediately aware of the absence of people out and about, so we ratcheted up our awareness level and continued to drive until we arrived in the heart of the village.

I was driving our Humvee and alternately scanning the rooftops and keeping an eye on the ANA light tactical vehicle (a lightly armored Ford Ranger) directly ahead of us. Losing contact with the vehicles in front of or behind you, known in Army jargon as a break in contact, is a recipe for disaster. Being alone, without the line-of-sight support of your fellow vehicles, makes you the lone target for the enemy. The ANA are notorious for driving at high speeds with little regard to maintaining a convoy's line-of-sight contact, so this is something you have to constantly watch.

Without warning, in the pickup directly in front of us, one of the ANA soldiers jumped up and squeezed off a barrage of AK rounds into an unseen target directly behind our Humvee. The whole convoy stopped, and the ANA, like sharks smelling blood in the water, all dismounted and began running back behind us, gunfire cracking around our Humvee all the while.

Uncertain as to what had happened, Ski spun the turret to our rear and I jumped out with my M4 rifle. The ANA were frantically pointing toward the compound behind us, but neither Ski nor I saw anyone, so we held our fire. Within minutes, the report made its way back to us that the soldier in the vehicle in front of us had seen a Taliban with a rocket-propelled grenade (RPG) rise up on the roof and aim at the rear of our vehicle. His quick response aborted the Taliban's attempt to destroy our Humvee, and the enemy soldier was felled by well-aimed gunshots to his leg, chest, and head. It was lucky for us, because at that close range we would have likely been injured or killed had he gotten his RPG shot off. The up-armored Humvee can normally take an RPG round, but at such close range, and targeted at our under-armored rear, it would have likely been game over for Ski and me.

Unfortunately, as is typical during such an ambush, the Taliban had well-planned escape routes. Despite aggressive pursuit by our ANA soldiers, the rest of the enemy managed to escape into surrounding compounds and alleyways.

Things settled down, and after consulting with the ANA commander, we agreed to consolidate our forces outside the village and continue the mission to our next objective. We moved our vehicle column to an open field, and thinking the enemy had fled, everyone let their guard down as we made our plan for the next village.

In hindsight, this was a *huge* mistake. Not long after consolidating everyone in the field, we started taking fire from a mud compound approximately two hundred meters to our north. We all took cover, and returned heavy fire, but the enemy was shooting through small slits in a long hundred-meter mud wall, which made hitting them nearly impossible. Nevertheless, the roar of our ETT and ANA machine guns was deafening and drowned out their AK fire.

After about ten minutes of this, things took a turn for the worse. We began taking AK and RPG fire from a similar walled compound about 150 meters directly to our south.

We found ourselves in a cross-fire ambush, and that's the worst place to be. We were out in the open, with only a handful of small well holes for cover. The ANA commander jumped into one of the holes, and the rest of the ANA soldiers followed suit. Ski and I found ourselves in an open area, unable to abandon our vehicle for better cover. While it was enticing to hide in a hole with the ANA, Ski, as the machine gunner, was the most powerful weapon we had currently engaging against those firing at us, and to abandon the gun goes against all rules of infantry combat. Likewise, the Humvee is our connection to the outside world through its radios, so leaving it was not an option until I let higher know where we were, and that we were pinned down and needed either CAS (close air support from Air Force planes or attack helicopters) or QRF (quick reaction force—basically reinforcements to come to our rescue).

So the bullets and RPGs were raining down on our forces. Ski and I could hear the near misses as the enemy bullets cracked past us. But Ski bravely remained in the turret, alternating his fire from the north to the south, keeping the enemy from advancing on our position and finishing us all off.

Our Afghan soldiers of Third Company, who are normally very brave, knew we were all in grave danger, but decided in this instance to follow the lead of their commander and hide in the holes. With few exceptions, they stopped engaging the enemy, and for about half an hour the only friendly forces returning fire on the enemy were Ski with his M240 Bravo and an occasional shot from my M4.

One drawback to having access to high-tech U.S. firepower (specifically CAS) is that the ANA is learning to expect this type of support. Unfortunately, it can take CAS support up to an hour to get to you, if you can get it at all. Planes may be involved in supporting other troops in other parts of the country, so it's hit or miss whether they will arrive to help.

I repeatedly told the ANA commander to have his forces return fire on the enemy, and maneuver toward their position to outflank them, and he was quick to respond, "No, you get planes and helicopters! They can kill the enemy."

Despite my numerous attempts to explain to him that this would take at least an hour, and we could all be dead by then, he stayed put in his hole and refused to maneuver his ANA forces. I found myself repeatedly running the gauntlet from our Humvee to his position, all the while facing enemy fire.

As if things couldn't get any worse, our radios stopped working, so my attempts to request CAS and QRF were ineffective and unsuccessful. But Ski, who remained in the gun turret of the Humvee, just kept firing our M240 Bravo, and his steady gunfire kept the enemy at bay.

Thinking that we had reached rock bottom, I was reminded by a Taliban RPG team that, indeed, things could be much worse. As I straddled the side of the Humvee, I heard the blast of an RPG being fired, and looked to the south to see the rocket heading directly at me and our Humvee. Luck intervened, and as the rocket ripped toward me, I noticed that the tail had a slight wobble that intensified as it flew closer, affecting its trajectory. Instead of slamming into me and the vehicle, it nose-dived and exploded into the field about fifteen meters directly in front of Ski and me. There was a cloud of dirt, flame, and fragmentation.

When the dust settled, I saw lying at my feet the metal ballast tube that holds the explosive football-shaped grenade. Ski and I were initially shocked by what had just happened, and as we looked at each other I screamed, "Holy shit! Did you see that RPG!" Ski, the true-blue infantryman, outdid my blasphemy with a hearty "Holy fuck!" Then we both grinned, happy to be alive, and turned our focus back to where the RPG had come from. Ski concentrated his machine-gun fire on the RPG team's position. He laid a good fifty to one hundred rounds into their position, and that was the last RPG that was fired at us during the engagement.

Within minutes, Ski was shot in the ear. The wound was superficial, but one inch to the right and he would have been killed. Again, disbelief on our part, followed by grins and more gunfire back at the enemy.

We remained in this holding pattern, me trying to make radio contact with our uncooperative radio, and Ski keeping the enemy from closing in on our position. Then, like the proverbial lightbulb going off in one's head, I remembered I had another tool I could use to get in touch with my head-quarters and request the needed CAS and QRF, something that I had completely forgotten about—a cell phone!

I quickly dialed up one of the officers in our headquar-ters, and got the War Eagle S3 (operations officer) on the phone. I gave him our current grid location and a brief expla-nation of our dire situation, and with this he went to work to get us some relief. Unfortunately, because the Humvee was armored, there was no reception from within its safer con-fines, so I had to stay outside to maintain cell phone contact, which further exposed me to the enemy fire. More cracking bullets, near misses, etc.

After almost an hour of being pinned down in this open field, we heard the distant rumble of aircraft, and within minutes, a B-1 bomber cruised overhead at an extremely low altitude. The intent was to scare off the Taliban. Our forces and the Taliban were too close to one another for the B-1 to drop any ordnance, so it was limited to a mission of intimidation. A five-hundred- or two-thousand-pound bomb, however accurate, would have affected us as much as the enemy, given our proximity.

While enemy fire did dissipate after the overflight of the B-1, they did not withdraw, and we remained stuck in the cross-fire ambush. To add insult to injury, the ANA com-mander yelled to me, "Why didn't it drop bombs!" I at-tempted to explain through my frazzled interpreter that any ordnance dropped had an equal chance of killing us as the enemy, but he refused to accept this answer. He continued to deny my requests that we maneuver out of the ambush area, despite my arguments. In the end, they were his ANA forces, not mine—he was the commander, and I was just an advisor, whose advice could be taken or rejected. In this case, it was repeatedly and heartily rejected.

The gunfire continued to taper down, and I heard my cell phone ring. A War Eagle ETT was on the line and reported that he had artillery lined up and ready to fire; all I had to do was adjust it onto the enemy. While this would have worked well, my concern was that the compounds were civilian, and although the enemy was using them, the chances of killing innocent Afghans who happened to be holed up there was too high, and I declined the artillery. At the time, this seemed like a commonsense decision. I put myself in the position of the families that owned these compounds. They would be killed, injured, or at the least homeless if artillery was used.

Finally, after about two hours of nerve-wracking combat, Coalition reinforcements arrived to the west of our position. When we saw the Humvees and Afghan pickups drive toward us, Polanski and I looked at each other and nervously laughed with relief. We couldn't believe we were still alive, and that neither of us had been seriously injured during two hours of intense enemy RPG and AK-47 fire.

I ran over to the first Humvee that arrived, expecting to see my familiar ETT soldiers. Instead, when I yanked open the Humvee door, a burly, unshaven Special Forces major stepped out. Surprised at this unexpected passenger, I inadvertently blurted out, "Who the hell are you?"

"I'm Major White with Task Force Paladin. What's the situation here?" he coolly responded.

"We've been surrounded and taking heavy fire for two hours."

"Surrounded?" A look of amusement rose on his face. "I *love* being surrounded!"

The QRF group, unofficially led by this Special Forces major, instantly changed the whole mood and morale of our ANA forces. As part of the QRF he brought a contingent of ANA soldiers led by an ANA officer known for bravery and sound tactical decisions. No longer was our hole-hugging ANA officer in charge.

The Special Forces major, along with the newly arrived ANA group, quickly drew up a plan and maneuvered out of the ambush area. They began patrolling the village, recapturing an ANA vehicle that had been taken by the Taliban during the initial ambush. They also moved on and outflanked the enemy's firing positions to our north. However, upon assaulting the compound, they discovered that the enemy had fled and was not to be found. They returned to our area, and with no enemy left on the battlefield and our ammo critically low, we all loaded up and began our movement back to our base.

Less than five minutes after leaving our initial ambush site, our convoy was attacked again. During this second engagement, Ski finally went blank on ammo, so our M240 Bravo gun was silenced. During the day it had fired almost one thousand rounds without malfunction, so it deserved a break from the action. We still had CAS on station, although the B-1 bomber had gone. Now it was a French Air Force Mirage burning holes in the sky. Unknown to us, it was already maneuvering to execute an overflight with the intent of identifying any enemy targets.

I say "unknown to us" because we never saw it coming. As we were firing at the enemy to our east, a terrifying blast ripped the air directly over us, and we were all pretty sure we had been hit by a rocket or an RPG.

After a few seconds of confusion and fear, we saw the French Mirage fighter jet tear past us at about fifty meters in the air (which is extremely low).

In jest, I yelled to Ski, "I think I just had a heart attack!"

But Ski wasn't in the mood for humor. "My legs are blown off!" he yelled in panic. The jet noise was so over-whelming and such a surprise that his legs had buckled under him, and for that brief moment he thought the Hum-vee had been hit by an RPG and his legs were gone. It was the first and only time I ever saw him scared in combat.

But Ski was in good company in his panic. I looked over at the Special Forces major, and he said with a grin, "I think I just crapped my pants!"

Andar, Ghazni Province. Vicinity of the 26 June first ambush site.

The Mirage must have had the same impact on the Taliban, as their firing ceased almost immediately. They likely deduced that the next overflight would drop a five-hundred-pound laser-guided bomb on their positions, so they packed up and withdrew. Again we mounted up our vehicles and headed toward Ring Road. An hour later, we returned to base, sore, fatigued, and still in awe at what we had survived.

27 JUNE: A CLEAR SHOT

When we arrived back at our ANA FOB, temperatures were still in the high nineties, and most of us were beyond dehydration. I remember stumbling into the TOC (tactical operations center) office and tossing my rifle, body armor, and helmet on the ground. Then I pretty much collapsed right there in the middle of the meeting room, spread-eagle on the floor.

Even though it was a first for someone to be laid out in the busy TOC, no one asked me what I was doing or why I was there. I alternated between mindlessly looking at the ceiling and rolling over and placing my blackened and dirty hands on my still sweaty face. I would remove them momentarily to stare at my hands. I felt like after thirty-seven years of life, I had just discovered they were attached to my body.

After about thirty minutes of this mental escapism, I mustered the emotional and physical energy for a phone call home. I crawled over to the table that held the satellite phone, reached up, and called my wife. I remember trying to impress on her how lucky I was to be alive. I should have died in that long ordeal of being surrounded, but the more I talked, the further I got from getting the point across. An RPG had me dead to rights. Due to some manufacturing defect, the tail-fin stabilizer didn't deploy, and it nose-dived into the ground in front of me, instead of hitting me.

My confused war-story carousel went round and round until she finally told me to go to bed. I don't remember anything else about my conversation with her, or even how I made it from the TOC to my room. I had mentally checked out well before my head hit my bed.

The next morning was 27 June. It started like every other one. Our adversaries in Andar permitted no rest for our weary bodies and shaky psyches. We had our regular ETT team meeting and went over the day's planned mission. There was another patrol scheduled into the same area where we had been ambushed three times the day before. The same undermanned and poorly planned mission was being run again with no interest from our operations officer in adjustments or analysis.

Fortunately, I wouldn't have to endure the bloodbath that was only hours away from occurring. I was physically sick, with an extreme case of diarrhea and dehydration, and mentally I was still rattled by the previous day's triple-header of combat. Given my condition, my commander said I was in no shape to go out on mission that day. But I felt a sense of guilt that I was being a pussy, and was sure all saw me as ducking my duty as a combat leader.

So Corporal Polanski, Captain Krow, and Captain Castro were selected as the crew for the sole up-armored Humvee going out on patrol that day. Within the hour, they linked up with the ANA company that would escort them and made their way down Ring Road toward Andar district.

Corporal Polanski had a habit of placing his digital camera on the small dashboard, aimed ahead to capture what he saw as he drove along. When he anticipated trouble, he would put it on movie mode and let it run. His two-gig memory card allowed for a good forty-five minutes of footage. Because of this practice, he captured some memorable moments and great audio of our combat engagements.

The transcript you are about to read is the audio, as recorded on his camera, from the final assault on a small Andar village, on 27 June 2006. In this attack, at least four Taliban were KIA. At least one was killed by Captain Krow and his M240 Bravo machine gun.

Setting up the scene is simple. Ski is the driver, Krow is in the turret manning the M240 Bravo machine gun, and Castro is commanding the vehicle, trying to manage the fight as best he can. Janis, the Afghan combat interpreter, sits in the backseat, communicating with the ANA on a handheld radio.

On the audio recording itself, the noises of the incoming and outgoing fire are deafening at times. Add to this the clunky hum of the Humvee engine, and the radio traffic squawking, and you can appreciate the confusion and perhaps understand the repetition of orders and comments passed among the crew of the Humvee.

Corporal Polanski is driving the vehicle out of a narrow alley on the outskirts of the village and Captain Krow is engaging some Taliban who are attempting to cross an open road. Ahead, about fifty meters, is an opening where ANA and ANP have set up a supporting fire position.

AUDIO STARTS:

(Heavy gunfire from the M240.)

Krow: "He went down!"

Ski: "Nice, you want me to go forward?"

(The M240 Bravo machine gun jams.)

Krow: "Fuck!"
Castro: "Yeah, yeah, go forward, see if we can go to an open field."
Krow: "He had a fucking weapon!"
Castro: "Okay, get to a fucking open field!"
Krow: "He went down, that's all I know."
Ski: "That's what's up!"
Castro: "You shot someone, you saw someone go down?"
Krow: "Yeah, I seen somebody fall down."
Castro: "Okay, then we gonna search in a minute over there."

(The vehicle starts moving forward toward the opening and the ANA and ANP soldiers.)

(Incoming gunfire is heard.)

(Vehicle stops near the opening.)

Krow: "Goddammit I don't have a shot here!"
Ski: "Backup?"
Castro: "Do you have a shot?"
Krow: "The wall's too high!"

(The vehicle creeps forward.)

Castro: "Can you see anything?"
Krow: "Trees are in my way!"
Castro: "The wall finishes over here, once the wall finishes you should have a clear shot."
Castro: "The ANP are calling us, go go go!"
Castro: "Do you have a clear shot now?"

Castro: "Get ready for it, get ready for it . . ."
Castro: "Here, you have a clear shot?"
Krow: "No, I don't have a clear shot!"

(ANP soldiers yelling in background.)

Krow: "What is he saying?"
Janis: "He is saying they [Taliban] are in the corner of that hill."
Castro: "Let's get over there then."
Ski: "Huh?"
Castro: "Go forward, and then turn to your left."
Janis: "One of the ANA is wounded."
Castro: "One is wounded?"
Ski :   "Where?"
Krow: "Right there!"
Ski: "Want me to give him first aid?"
Castro: "Yeah, fuck the risk."
Janis: "Don't go out there, they [Taliban] are in front of us there!"
Krow: "He's right behind us!"
Castro: "Wounded . . ."

(Audio is disrupted by a near-miss explosion of an RPG aimed at the Humvee.)

Krow: "Goddammit."
Ski: "Yo, I'm getting the fuck out of here!"
Ski: "You want me to go forward?"
Krow: "You need to either go backward or forward!"

(Vehicle starts moving forward.)

Castro: "Right here."
Krow: "STOP!"
Castro: "You got a clear shot? Go for it!"

(Long bursts of M240 machine-gun fire.)

Krow: "I'm out!"

(Reloading noises—ammo cans clanking.)

(Continued M240 Bravo fires, as well as incoming shots.)

Castro: "The ANA is moving, fire fire!"

(Audio disrupted from another RPG explosion near Humvee.)

Krow: "See that wall, they are right in there!"
Ski: "I wish I had a fucking 203 [grenade launcher]!"

(Incoming enemy AK-47 and RPK machine-gun fire.)

Krow: "Where the fuck did that come from?"
Castro: "Where is the guy that's wounded?"
Krow: "He's right back there, he's sitting there on the side of the road!"
Ski: "Get me the [medical aid] bag quick, I'm gonna run!"
Ski: "Get me the bag!"
Krow: "Hang on, I'll cover you!"
Ski: "Start shooting!"

(Extensive incoming/outgoing fire as Ski exits the vehicle and runs back to treat the wounded ANA soldier.)

(Gunfire.)

(Gunfire.)

(RPG explosion.)

AUDIO ENDS.

Corporal Polanski and members of Third Company 2/1/203, on 27 June,
shortly after driving the Taliban from the village.

Postscript: CPT Krow was severely injured by an RPG
weeks later, within kilometers of this 27 June 2006 engagement. He was in Afghanistan for only six weeks before he
was evacuated back to Walter Reed for extensive surgeries
and rehabilitation.

DECENCY

The TIC (troops in combat) event of 27 June did not culminate on the battlefield. The emotional effects of that day played out into the evening, long after the dead had been collected and the guns had been silenced. As described, I had been kept back due to diarrhea and dehydration. During one of the many trips to the latrine that day, I stood on the scale and realized I had lost twenty-five pounds in six weeks.

When I heard the rumble of the Humvee returning from the daylong mission, I left my hooch to help Ski, Krow, and Castro download their gear and weapons. Ski was clearly not in a talkative mood, so I gave him space. When I saw him twenty minutes later in our kitchen, I approached him to get debriefed on how things had gone. The radio traffic throughout the day had been a constant running gunfight. It had been a tough day for all.

As I got close to him, I noticed his uniform sleeves were covered in blood, dirt, and gore. His normal upbeat and vulgar disposition was absent. He sat down and began to tell me about the mission, as I collected some food items and cooked him a quick dinner—ramen noodles and peanut butter on Afghan naan bread.

Normally, he would have made his own selection, but he was in no mood to cook. He could barely manage to light his cigarette. The "thousand-yard stare" was in full effect. He was clearly still out on the battlefield, reliving the various what-ifs that had played out earlier in the day.

The story started predictably: Taliban ambush, returned fire, RPGs, near misses. As the engagement developed, Ski and the two captains riding in the Humvee were firing on, and receiving AK and RPG fire from, Taliban soldiers in a small village.

After some heavy fire from the ETTs, ANP, and ANA soldiers, they maneuvered into the village and immediately came across a handful of wounded and dead Taliban. Some lay dead where they fell, others had crawled into shallow ditches and lay there dying. The combined fire from the friendly forces had been so fierce that the Taliban had abandoned their wounded. It's worth mentioning that this is extremely uncommon. After we engaged them in combat we normally found only blood trails, discarded sandals, and disheveled turbans, never any wounded or dead.

Ski is normally an infantry gun-bunny killing machine. He chomps at the bit before each mission, hoping we will encounter the enemy. He is not one to wax humanistic or show compassion in response to the suffering we see daily. His normal answer to most questions about the Taliban is, "Kill them all."

But Ski, upon seeing the wounded Taliban, immediately grabbed his combat lifesaver medical bag and moved to begin treating. Doing this was a risk to his own life: the enemy was still in the area, and the wounded lay in ditches in an open road. Yet without hesitation, he used his limited remaining medical supplies on the enemy, in an attempt to give them comfort and aid.

He described to me, while he ate the food I prepared for him, how one of the injured Taliban was going into shock—his femoral artery had been hit and he was bleeding out. "This guy was looking at me with fear in his eyes, expecting me to finish him off. When he realized I was trying to stop his bleeding, he relaxed and put his hand over his heart." In Afghanistan, it's customary among men to put a hand over the heart as a sign of deep respect and thanks.

The poignancy of this scene is unparalleled. Here is a Taliban man dying, felled by our bullets, showing a final act of thanks for this decent treatment. And there is Ski, the

Corporal Polanski (left) and Captain Castro treat a wounded Taliban soldier, who died shortly after this photo was taken.

brutal warrior, holding this man in his arms, trying to make his final moments as comfortable and painless as possible.

This image of compassion from an unlikely source, in an unlikely place, is stuck in my head. As I sat there and listened to Ski, coated with the enemy's blood, I knew this day would stay with him for the rest of his life. It's a small—but tangible—example of decency and honor in an environment full of hate and pain.

MINES

Improvised explosive devices (IEDs) are the weapon of choice for the enemy in Afghanistan. More soldiers are killed and wounded by these high-tech booby traps than by any other weapon.

In Ghazni, however, the summer of 2006 was relatively IED-free. In late May, a huge blast leveled a mosque within the city proper. Evidence at the blast site suggested that the complete Ghazni IED manufacturing cell was killed by the explosion while practicing their deadly craft.

But as the summer wore on, this stroke of good fortune did not result in a reduction of threats to our vehicles while moving along the roads. Instead of emplacing IEDs, the enemy went to their plan B: a seemingly endless supply of Italian pressure-plate antitank mines left over from the Russian war.

Mines, in my opinion, are the most terrifying weapon we faced in Afghanistan. IED devices can be jammed by our electronic warfare countermeasures, and sometimes they fail to go off due to poor construction or emplacement. But the pressure-plate mine is a sure thing if a vehicle rolls over it, and the damage can be catastrophic. The other reason why I fear mines is because they allow for no warning against the impact. With gunfire and RPGs, there is usually an audible warning of the incoming rounds, and a split second to duck, flinch, or shield one's face and vitals. But mines provide no warning—just an instantaneous blast of incredible force and pressure.

The roads throughout Ghazni Province are dirt, rock, and sand. There is one paved highway, the Ring Road, but we traveled almost exclusively on unimproved bone-jarring wadis and goat trails, which allow for easy concealment and emplacement of mines.

Every drive into the back country of the province is a white-knuckle experience. And luck is a bigger factor than skill in finding an emplaced mine before it finds you. Occasionally, an amateur emplaces a mine, and we can see the uneven color and texture of the disturbed earth and avoid it. But this is the exception to the norm. The vast majority of mines during this summer in Ghazni were discovered "the hard way."

In July, our whole ANA battalion and ETT team went out on an urgent mission to recapture an ANA light tactical vehicle that had been captured by the Taliban. The last known location, as reported to us through our informant network, was in the heart of Andar district. As we moved deeper into Andar, our long convoy was stopped by a freak downpour. It hadn't rained in months, and now it came down in sheets for about twenty minutes.

Unknown to us, a squad of Taliban were using this halt in our movement to plant an antitank mine in our path and to lay a secondary ambush on us. Once the rain lifted, the lead vehicles began their forward movement. Within minutes, from our position at the rear of the convoy, we experienced what I would describe as a "flash-bang." It seemed like it took long seconds for the comprehension of what had occurred to register, but a shock wave and deafening noise removed any lingering confusion.

Then the denial sets in. That blast can't be what I think it is. The mind revolts at the grotesque images of human bodies exposed to such a force.

Time slows, then speeds up. The next thing I remember are desperate orders screamed on the radio for our vehicle to move up to the explosion site. We had an Army nurse, Captain Komar, on board our Humvee. He was the only medical member of our ETT team, and he was needed immediately at the blast site. So we began our movement up the convoy. As we got closer, the staccato of machine-gun fire could be heard, as well as the blast of RPGs. The Taliban in Andar were infamous for mine-initiated ambushes, and my heart sank knowing we were driving full speed ahead into one.

We finally made a slight turn and came upon an opening. In the middle of it sat the destroyed ANA pickup. It was turned sideways, and the front third of the vehicle was gone. Dancing from left to right all around the destroyed vehicle were red and green tracer rounds.

A two-sided ambush had been emplaced, and was sprung only after the first responders had approached the damaged vehicle to treat the wounded. At that moment, Captain Komar was the bravest man in Afghanistan. While I pondered the wisdom of driving into an open area to extract the wounded, he had already put his foot on the gas pedal and went screaming into the fray.

As we approached the vehicle, the deep bass blast of an RPG went off to our left, which had me screaming profanities as fast as they came to mind. Komar positioned the

This is the ANA Ford Ranger that hit the Taliban emplaced mine. Captain Komar dragged the wounded ANA soldier from the driver-side door while under fire from the mud compounds in the background of the photo.

Humvee so that it was shielding the destroyed vehicle from the right side, where most of the fire was coming from. Ski was on the gun, methodically laying suppressive fire along the tops of the walls the Taliban were firing from.

Komar dismounted and checked to see if anyone was alive. By a miracle, the two ANA soldiers who were in the vehicle were alive, albeit mangled. I knew things were bad when I saw the look on Komar's face as he first surveyed the carnage. He yelled to me, "This guy has his legs on backwards!"

The driver had multiple compound femur fractures and a foot that was wedged in the twisted metal of the vehicle. It was a difficult task for Komar to extricate him, especially while under fire. The second soldier was blinded by some serious cuts to his eyes. One eyeball was split in half. To keep things interesting, the enemy decided to fire more RPGs from our left, and Ski quickly rotated the gun turret and shifted fire onto their positions.

Through the bravery of Captain Komar and the heavy M240 Bravo machine-gun fire from Ski, SFC Deghand, Captain Cain, and our ANA, the patients were removed and pulled back to a safe area without any further injury. The battle continued for another ten minutes before the enemy withdrew. Captain Komar stabilized the wounded, and about an hour later they were flown out via Blackhawk helicopter.

The ETTs went about checking ammo, and accounted for all our U.S. and ANA personnel and equipment. The decision was made to continue our march deeper into Andar, and by noon, a long column of vehicles and soldiers began moving down the road. More mines and more ambushes would await us that day, but none would inflict any further casualties or damage to our equipment. Our nerves, however, had been thoroughly rattled.

PINK MIST

All was quiet in the War Eagle ETT tactical operations center. Two of our ETT teams and two ANA platoons had deployed to search a couple of towns in Andar district about two hours earlier, and all was proceeding without incident.

At about 1030 hours, jumbled and broken radio traffic filled the TOC. The unwelcome message was of an ambush and ETT wounded. The Taliban had surrounded an ETT team of two and a small group of ANA who were separated from their main group.

Then the radio went silent. Shock filled the room. Everyone tried to maintain a look of composure, but the emotional wheels were spinning wildly in our heads. I started to clean an M240 Bravo machine gun in hopes it would prevent anyone from seeing how badly my hands were shaking.

The most difficult thing about such a situation is that no one knows the details. It's like being told your father was just in a car accident. Was it a fender bender, or a lethal head-on collision? The mind fills the void with the worst possible images and pictures. And not knowing how bad the injury was to our ETT teammate was paralyzing.

A quick reaction force was spun up to help our guys fight out of their dilemma—assuming they were still alive by the time we could get there. And that was the concern we all had running through our heads as we prepped the QRF. It wouldn't take long for a Taliban force to wipe out such a small group, especially with one of the two ETTs wounded. Within ten minutes, the QRF was tearing down Ring Road toward the last known location of our besieged forces in Andar.

1100 hours: More radio traffic fills our TOC. A medevac request is relayed to higher from a sister U.S. element in the area. That's good news. It means the wounded are still alive, and were able to communicate with someone about their situation. But the feeling of helplessness remains. There are too many unknown variables, and a lot can transpire on the battlefield in an hour. Wounded can expire; more casualties can be sustained, etc. Having completed cleaning the M240 Bravo, I sit in the TOC with my head in my hands, making small talk as we all try to reassure each other that everything will be okay.

1205 hours: More bits and pieces of information on the radio from the U.S. forces in the area. We now know the location of the ambush, that there are a lot of enemy fighters, and that our wounded were injured by a direct RPG-7 hit. The RPG is a shoulder-fired rocket-propelled grenade, which literally can tear open an armored vehicle and reduce soldiers to large chunks.

1210 hours: Our ETT is still alive, although he has sustained wounds that required three tourniquets. Not good—morale sinks. Also, the combat interpreter accompanying them has been confirmed to be injured, but no information about severity is provided.

1255 hours: Finally, a radio message from Captain Cain, the sole uninjured ETT present during the ambush. They are en route to the U.S. base to link up with the air medevac, which will take our wounded to a higher medical hospital for immediate treatment.

1305 hours: Our wounded ETT is on the bird, alive, conscious, and stable. He has sustained serious frag wounds from the RPG to his side, and one of his legs is nearly amputated, but still attached. This is *great news*. Morale in our TOC jumps, and hugs and high fives are passed around. Any infantryman can tell you that it's better to be alive without a leg than KIA on the battlefield with your limbs still attached. Also, we hear our interpreter did not require evacuation via air, which means his injuries are not severe.

1420 hours: The QRF returns, and Vandy and I are tasked with cleaning out the Humvee used to transport our wounded. Pools of blood are visible on the seat, and splashes of reddish brown are all over the side of the vehicle. The stretcher requires extensive cleaning, and we wash and scrub off clots, skin chunks, and a lot of deep red blood from the dark green canvas.

1530 hours: Our ETT is in surgery on the other side of the country. Prognosis is mixed for him to keep his leg, but it's too early to tell. From Captain Cain, we begin to get details about what had happened.

While establishing a blocking position, the two ETTs and a squad of ANA were ambushed from compound rooftops. The first shot, which was a good one, sent an RPG skidding on the ground and up under the Humvee. The wounded ETT had dismounted and was standing next to the vehicle. Fortunately, the majority of the fragmentation from the RPG was contained in the underbody of the Humvee. Cain, who was the gunner in the turret, armed with a Mark

Cain, War Eagle ETT.

19 automatic grenade launcher, immediately returned fire.
He went through all his ammo, keeping the Taliban from
moving in closer to finish off the semi-surrounded forces.
He transitioned to his M4 rifle, expending all his basic ammo
load, then dismounted and grabbed the injured ETT's rifle,
and went through hundreds more .223 rounds. His timing
was perfect, as the turret of the Humvee was hit by enemy
fire just as he left it.

Those who live by the sword die by the sword, and Captain Cain killed the RPG gunner, as well as another Taliban
who exposed himself a bit too long. He also killed two Taliban when he was firing the Mark 19. The proximity of the
enemy was such that when Captain Cain was firing his M4
carbine, he was able to see what we refer to as "the pink
mist," the fine spray of blood and brains from the high-

velocity M4 bullet passing through the skull. In this case, revenge was a dish served hot.

Captain Cain's steady fire kept the Taliban from overrunning his small perimeter and prevented any further injuries to friendly forces. Approximately three weeks after this engagement, we received information that one of the Taliban's key leaders in this area had been injured in this fight, and had died of his wounds en route to Pakistan. He was being transported for medical treatment after being shot by Captain Cain.

NIGHT LETTERS

The people awake to the warm, dusty air of Ghazni. The call to prayer stirs them from their slumber, as the sun begins to rise and build upon the heat from the day before. Male voices emanate from old loudspeakers propped on mosque walls across the city. This is the starting rhythm of daily life all across Afghanistan, the delivery of a traditional religious offering heard throughout the land for hundreds of years.

But on this morning, the call to prayer is only one of the messages the people of Ghazni have waiting for them. Greeting them on this hot, dusty morning, nailed to doors, and scattered in the streets, are photocopied messages from an unknown and unseen deliveryman.

Night letters.

These photocopied papers carry an ominous and anonymous threat. Death awaits anyone who works with, works for, or supports the Government of Afghanistan or the Coalition Forces. Police, soldiers, interpreters, contractors, and laborers are featured prominently on the list of targets.

The myriad of gruesome threats vary with each letter, but the warning remains the same: Cooperate or collaborate with the government, and you will die.

Terror in Afghanistan need not be delivered through explosions or gunfire. Words can suffice, and these night letters put Afghans in a difficult spot. The economy here is broken; jobs are few and far between, and there are many mouths to feed at home. The Coalition pays wages much higher than those created by the indigenous economy. The Army, police, and other government agencies do not pay well, but at least provide a guaranteed income and some economic stability.

So now it comes down to the simple question: Is your life worth this risk? Is providing for your family going to outweigh the risk to your life? Forget for a moment the Afghan context—how would *you* respond if you awoke to a letter nailed to your door that said if you continued to work for your current employer, you would be killed?

This summer in Ghazni, an Afghan National Police officer who was killed in combat with the Taliban was buried in the local cemetery. The next morning his body was found, exhumed by the Taliban, with a night letter nailed to his forehead.

They drove home their message, literally, with a hammer and a carpenter's nail: the wages of cooperation are indeed the wages of death.

THE WEAPON WITH NO BULLETS

There is no shortage of lethal combat power in our ANA-ETT forces. From small arms, to crew-served weapons, to artillery and close air support, we can summon incredible kinetic force on the battlefield, with pinpoint accuracy and effect. But ironically, our most important weapon has no bullets or munitions to speak of.

It is my opinion that this war cannot and will not be won militarily. That is not to say it shouldn't be fought, because it should. But victory, however you define it, will come when the Afghan government is capable of providing security and some semblance of prosperity and welfare for the people, not because we have killed all the Taliban.

And that is where our non-kinetic secret weapon comes into play. On our FOB, open to the public at designated hours, is a free medical clinic staffed and run by ANA personnel, and supervised by Captain Komar, the Army nurse. Its open-door policy allows anyone, regardless of income, allegiance, social status, or residency, to come and receive free medical care.

FOB Ghazni sign welcoming all patients to the free medical clinic run by Captain Komar and ANA medical personnel.

Captain Komar confers with a local villager seeking medical assistance at the ANA medical clinic.

For most Afghans, health care here is a luxury, and given the economic condition of the country, health care remains inaccessible to almost all. But here at our ANA-run medical clinic, they are given free care; and prescriptions, if they are in supply, are also free. It's fast and efficient. The average stay is no more than thirty minutes, and that includes check-in, the doctor's visit, and the filling of prescriptions. The lack of paperwork or liability considerations would make an American doctor jealous of how simple and fast the system here works.

I frequently remind my infantry soldiers of Third Company that even though we are badass Taliban hunters, and we have the power to destroy any enemy that we find, medical clinic remains our most powerful weapon in winning this war. If we could build a clinic like this in the heart of every Taliban area, it would do more to win popular support than any presence patrol or combat operation to root out Taliban fighters. Our ANA FOB has yet to be directly attacked, while the U.S. FOB just two kilometers down the road is the regular recipient of rockets and gunshots. We feel this has something to do with the clinic, and that even the Taliban know it's a valuable resource that should be kept intact. Even the Taliban's children get sick and need care, and they recognize this.

A medical clinic is the keystone to success in Afghanistan.

A CUT THROAT

E ven during periods of relative peace and quiet, the war finds ways to creep into your personal space and violate your growing false sense of security.

Late one night, while going to snag a cold bottle of Gatorade out of the fridge in our TOC, my attention was diverted from my thirst by frantic voices coming over the radio.

Somewhere, out in the darkness, in some valley, at some random grid square, ETTs were in a bad firefight. The urgency, the terror, the frantic tones of their voices had a paralyzing effect on me. The bottle of Gatorade became heavy, and it fell from my hands onto the floor. I immediately had a sense of being alone, vulnerable, helpless.

Flashbacks to moments when I've found myself outflanked, outmaneuvered, outnumbered, and under fire. The hot summer night instantly felt cold, and I literally shook. As difficult as it was to stay and listen to desperate calls and orders on the radio, especially alone, I couldn't move. I had become part of their world.

Normally, Army radio transmissions are very formal and programmed. But when things go bad, it's all out the window. And things had gone bad.

"Keep your eyes on that fucking wall . . . He's there! He's there!"

The staccato of an M240 Bravo machine gun ripped the radio speakers.

Voices faltered, quavered; strong men were choking on their words.

"Fucking shoot them! Fucking shoot them!"

Then silence. Nothing.

I don't know how the battle ended. I ran out of the TOC. I couldn't handle it, and being in there alone was too much for me. I nervously laughed at myself as I ran in the darkness back to my hooch, half mocking my childish fear, half running from something I felt was pursuing me.

But you can't run away from the war.

The night passed. The sun rose. All was apparently well again in the world. When I returned to the TOC in the morning, the radio squawked with normal administrative chatter of movements, reports, and updates. The TOC was filled with teammates and the usual upbeat and boisterous banter.

Relaxed, I joined in on this small talk with my teammates. Yet, when I heard a report come over the radio that an ANA soldier had been killed the night before in that fight, I immediately was carried back to that feeling of terror.

The dead ANA soldier had been found, his throat cut, and his body booby-trapped with explosives. Alone.

I was glad I had run through the darkness.

ROCKETS

One of the methods the Taliban like to use to kill us is rocket attacks on our FOB. They have many techniques and tactics to aim and fire these things at us. The bad news is that rockets are lethal and easily launched, and the Taliban seem to have a never-ending supply of them. The good news is that the rockets are unguided, and frequently sail harmlessly over our FOBs, blowing up in empty fields.

However, the law of averages says that if you fire enough of them, you'll eventually hit something. This week, Ski and I found ourselves visiting the Ghazni PRT to meet with SSG Phaneuf to get our radios fixed. He is the commo god in these parts, and if we can't fix it, he can. We also had to get some maintenance done on our up-armored Humvee, and the PRT is the place for that, too. Standing by the vehicle, donning our body armor for the trip back to our ANA FOB, we hear a "shhhh" noise of something flying through the air, quickly followed by an explosion. In this case, the bad guys did a good job of aiming their rocket, and actually hit the FOB. Ski and I each jumped in the Humvee like a little kid would jump into his mother's arms for protection.

Even though the rockets are highly inaccurate, they still do a number on the nerves. It's a weapon that you really can't do anything to avoid—you can't outrun them, so if it's aimed at you, it's just your bad luck. Additionally, they usually come at night when you're sleeping, so that can mess your sleep up if you start thinking too much about it.

This rocket attack that Ski and I witnessed jarred my nerves a bit, but I'm pretty sure it freaked Ski out more than me, because he has had worse rocket experiences lately. Just yesterday, Ski and Vandy were back at the PRT, and a rocket landed about thirty meters in front of them, careened off the side of the PRT TOC, and then spun around until it fizzled out. For whatever reason, the rocket never detonated.

A couple months ago, Ski was taking a shower when he

Rocket shrapnel that hit the front door and wall of Ski's barracks.

heard an explosion, and quickly finished up. When he was returning to his barracks, he heard another explosion behind him. It turns out the first blast he had heard hit the front of his barracks while he was in the shower, and the second hit the shower when he was returning to his barracks. Suffice to say, neither Ski nor I are looking for any more rocket experiences in the near future.

CHANCE

We are at the end of a long night of patrols and never-ending missions in hot pursuit of fleeing Taliban, who have wiggled out of the jaws of Operation Mountain Fury. Adrenaline only takes you so far, and the body revolts, demanding sleep.

As the driver of his up-armored Humvee, Ski is burned out, and a rest halt is called. The patrol's vehicles stop and form up a "strongpoint" defensive position. The weary crews bed down on the dirt, the hoods, and in the turrets for some much-needed sleep.

The commander decides to exempt all drivers from pulling security during the night, to maximize their ability to safely drive another long day without risk of a sleep-deprivation accident. Ski is happy. He's out like a light.

Blackness.

Interrupted by a hand shaking his shoulder. "Corporal, get up. It's your guard shift!"

Ski rises, about to coldcock this soldier for waking him up, but being the guy he is, Ski sucks it up, crawls out of his sleeping bag, and gets up in the turret. Pissed, but like I said, a team player. So he does it.

The sun's gloomy light slowly climbs into the sky. Ski continues his vigil. The ANA begin stirring, and an ANA soldier brings him *chai* (tea). Vehicles and crews start coming back to life.

Ski, to retrieve his cigarette lighter, drops down from the turret into the vehicle for an instant. And it's an instant that saves his life.

Three simultaneous explosions, blended into one deafening blast of air and noise and shrapnel, rip apart an ANA vehicle not more that ten meters away. Chunks of shrapnel screech through the airspace his head had occupied seconds earlier.

This picture of Corporal Polanski was taken hours after the explosions described in this essay.

To add insult to injury, his sleeping bag, where he should still be dreaming away, is punctured and perforated by hot metal chunks and silvery shards.

And the soldier who brought him tea moments ago now moans in shock, legs torn off and twisted, an arm burned and deformed. His remaining fingers point in unnatural positions; incoherent cries to Allah are uttered from his burned throat for ringing ears to hear.

This is perhaps the most vibrant example of *inshallah*—*"God's will."* The accidental wake-up call, the choice to duck in the turret at the precise second of the explosion. These ingredients breed life and second chances, while destroying others without reason.

AN ORANGE-BEARDED MAN

Yesterday, a group of Taliban attacked the district center town of Disi in our area of operations, and unfortunately killed a young Afghan policeman during the attack. He was a teenager and a new recruit to the ANP. Most people who join the ANP get little training and are under-armed and isolated in small groups as they patrol the wild lands of Ghazni Province. It's normal for ANP stations and patrols to be attacked by large bands of better-armed Taliban. A large portion of ANA missions in Ghazni are in support of overwhelmed ANP units in contact.

Our ETT and ANA forces received word that this distant village was under attack, and that the ANP needed support. We mounted up our Humvees, bristling with heavy crew-served weapons, and drove through the countryside for hours until we arrived at the village of Disi. When all was said and done, the ANP had received reinforcements from other ANP stations before we arrived, and the Taliban had fled. Some Taliban had been captured during their retreat, and as related, one policeman was killed in the firefight.

Our role in Disi was limited to reestablishing a sense of calm and control in the town.

Given the lack of hostilities, I relaxed in the turret of my Humvee and took in the scenery of the village, watching it slowly return to normal. Goatherds were moving their flocks through the streets back to the fields to graze. Children were returning to the streets from the safe confines of their mud-walled compounds. Elders had gathered in the shade along the side of a mud wall, and were forcefully questioning ANP and ANA officers about their plans to better protect their village from this disruption.

Among this buzz of increasing activity, an old man caught my attention. What I first noticed was his bright orange beard, recently dyed with henna. The second thing that I couldn't ignore was his voice. He was wailing and moaning, and was increasingly drowning out the background noises of the village. He wandered from group to group, first to the elders, then the soldiers, then the police. He moaned and yelled to anyone who would listen.

No one did. So he continued on his way through the village. He wandered through the growing mass of people, back and forth, by my position. Even though he was physically surrounded by people, he remained very much alone in his angst and emotion.

To me, as a soldier, his erratic behavior was both alarming and disarming. In the end, I saw no weapons on him, nor lumps in his clothing to suggest a suicide vest. I ultimately deemed him too crazy to be a threat, and ignored him.

But this thin, weathered man, with his festive orange beard, wasn't interested in leaving, and continued seeking answers to his distressed questions, growing more emotional and erratic with each shout.

The Americans present, by now, had all concluded that

My view from the gun turret in Disi, moments before the arrival of the orange-bearded man.

he was the village idiot. We eventually came to laugh at his antics. We joked about him among ourselves to pass the remaining hours that we stood guard in the village. Only upon our mounting up to leave Disi did we find out the reason for his histrionics. The old man with the orange beard was the father of the young policeman killed earlier in the day. Our laughter was immediately replaced by regret. We all left Disi feeling like shit for mocking him in his most painful moment.

THE GARDEN OF EDEN MASSACRE
(ALMOST)

Hidden in an expanse of barren, inhospitable mountains and dry desert valleys lies what can only be described as the Afghan Garden of Eden. It's not on any map, and you'd have a difficult time finding it if you were looking for it because it fits neatly within a one-kilometer grid square. I'm convinced most outsiders find it more by accident than on purpose. After hours of driving through desolate and sparsely populated wastelands, we stumbled upon it: a green, fertile patch of paradise.

The richness of this field of green was matched only by the variety of animals populating it. Like a staging area for Noah's ark, it had animals at every pond and patch of grass. Horses, cattle, water buffalo, camels, sheep, goats, and purebred Afghan hounds. All were peacefully feeding or resting in this expanse of green comfort.

And it was this green paradise, populated by such a peaceful gathering of four-legged creatures, that through confusion and misdirection almost became the site of a massacre of hundreds of innocent civilians. Had this carnage occurred, it would have been front-page news around the world, the Afghan version of Vietnam's My Lai Massacre. And who would have been identified as the mastermind, the bloody, coldhearted murderer who worked efficiently to kill hundreds? Who would replace the infamous Lieutenant Calley as the embodiment of outrage against the innocent?

Me.

The local Pashtun villagers in this Afghan Garden of Eden, among all these animals existing so peacefully, had introduced rules that unintentionally would start a series of bloody events. These events would shortly bring me into the position of unknowingly ordering a massacre of the innocent.

It all started when a horse wandered away from its master and trespassed into the land of nutritious grasses and clear water. In previous days, a large tribe of Cuchie nomads had moved into the area bordering the valley, and one of their livestock wandered off, drawn by the sweet, humid smells of green grass and warm, shallow ponds.

The mostly Pashtun tribes, for whom this valley was a permanent home, were not happy about the new Cuchie presence, but they accepted it as a natural part of the cycle of life here in Afghanistan. Like the rising and setting sun, Cuchies had moved through these mountains for generations, with a seasonal predictability. But the invasion of their green watering hole by a Cuchie animal was not going to be tolerated. The wayward horse was confiscated, and before long, Cuchies had entered the Pashtun village seeking the release of their property.

Given the cultural need for honor and respect, and the presence of many AK-47s among the Pashtun and Cuchie groups, the attempted repossession of the wayward horse quickly escalated into a violent scene. Who said what or did what during these tense moments is unclear. But when the dust settled, empty bullet casings littered the streets, hostages had been taken by both sides, and a small Pashtun boy lay dead, struck by an errant bullet.

Both sides in this tribal conflict collapsed back into defensive positions—the Cuchies spread along the lower-elevation plateaus of the mountain, and the Pashtuns holed up in their village. Both sides preferred defense to offense, and they spent the next twenty-four hours preparing for the worst.

The next day saw maneuvering in both the mountain and the villages. The Cuchies, who despite their nomadic and minimalist lifestyle are renowned arms dealers and smugglers, dug in defensive positions on the mountain, and produced, seemingly out of thin air, medium machine guns, small arms, and RPGs. Rumors of a Cuchie Dyshka, a heavy machine gun capable of shooting down helicopters and slow-moving aircraft, circulated in the surrounding Pashtun villages.

Not to be outdone, the Pashtuns, aware of an uneven and unfavorable distribution of firepower, used their time-tested cunning and decided to bring in some allies to balance out the uneven force of arms. The Pashtun elders made contact with the regional ANP unit and delivered a message that was as urgent as it was false. These elders had a story they knew the police couldn't resist: "This is *not* a tribal dispute. There are four hundred Taliban in the mountains next to our village. *Help!*"

The ANP had only one reaction to this startling information. They didn't have the forces to take on four hundred dug-in Taliban. With the enemy in such numbers, this fight would require the ANA, and ultimately the Americans. They immediately started getting out word that they needed support.

Back at our ETT tactical operations center in Ghazni, I overheard my team chief discussing some tribal conflict out west in an area we didn't even have maps posted for. It would take another day before the Taliban twist on the story would make it to our TOC. It would take two more days before I was in the position to unintentionally kill hundreds of civilians.

When the ANA formally received word of this new development—the presence of a large Taliban force—they sent a platoon of their soldiers west, where they linked up with the ANP. The officer in charge, both brave and stubborn, decided to test the validity of the Pashtun elders' story. It is worth noting that reports of "hundreds of Taliban" are common, and are almost always wildly inaccurate. The ANA commander on the ground was skeptical that there would be such a high concentration of enemy in such a remote location.

It was this skepticism and doubt that allowed the ANA commander to execute a direct attack on four hundred alleged Taliban with only thirty soldiers. The Cuchies, expecting the police and Army to come as neutral negotiators, instead found themselves under fire by these very forces, and responded with their equally impressive firepower. The Cuchies quickly repelled the police and Army forces, and inflicted numerous wounds among the ANA and ANP soldiers. One ANP soldier was shot in his groin area, resulting in the violent and instant removal of his testicles from his body. Even more disturbing was one ANP soldier killed in the short-lived and unsuccessful assault.

This foiled attack by the ANA and ANP did accomplish one thing. It proved beyond a doubt that there were hostile and well-armed forces on the mountain. A call back to Ghazni was made for more reinforcements. This time, we would be joining a larger force of ANA on the long, dusty drive to the now "confirmed Taliban" mountain stronghold. The next morning, two ETT gun trucks would join the ANA reinforcements as they drove west toward what was shaping up to be a large-scale battle.

After about five hours of bone-jarring driving through rocky, desolate terrain, I remember turning a corner around a large rock formation and seeing an incredible vista of green. The collection of animals, the smell of damp earth, the vibrant shades of plant life were pleasant and breathtaking. We didn't have too much time to marvel at the spectacle, because we quickly climbed a small hill, and the Afghan Garden of Eden was gone from view. On the other side of this small hill lay the first of the Pashtun villages. Within minutes we had arrived at our objective, a rudimentary village center. It featured a gas station that had no gas pumps, only a handful of old plastic bottles filled with gasoline, lined up on the ground in front of a simple mud-constructed building. There was also an Afghan version of a corner store that sold some locally made snacks, candies, and sodas. Last was the medical clinic, which the ANA and ANP had made their command post. It was a fitting location for their headquarters, as it allowed them to monitor the status of their wounded, who lay inside the clinic in varying states of pain and consciousness. To the north, approximately five kilometers away, stood in full view the enormous and wide-based mountain containing the alleged enemy fighters.

Our first task upon arrival was to coordinate medevac of the wounded ANA and ANP soldiers. U.S. helicopters will not land unless there are U.S. personnel on the ground to confirm the wounded, the injuries, and the safety and security of the site. Now that we were on the ground, Captain Cain, my ETT teammate, began coordination of this mission, and within an hour the wounded ANA and ANP were loaded on a Blackhawk and outbound for treatment at a U.S. base.

As the helicopter made its way south, escorted by an Apache attack helicopter, it was clear that the sun was also an opponent for us, as we only had a couple hours of daylight to work with. Night would create an opportunity for this enemy horde to escape, and we knew that with the medevac helicopters' visible presence, the enemy knew the Americans had arrived.

With my interpreter by my side, I collected the stories from the Pashtun elders, who made a convincing case for the danger posed by the Taliban in the mountains. Captain Cain also met with the ANP and ANA leadership, as well as more village elders. The story was the same from all quarters. There were Taliban. There were lots of them. And now with the arrival of the American ETTs, it was time to commence a much more lethal level of hostilities.

I got on the radio to my TOC and relayed the information from the scene. All signs pointed to an incredibly lucky opportunity to kill a lot of Taliban, as they regrouped and rearmed themselves in this heretofore unknown mountain base camp. The Pashtun elders personally told me stories of Taliban groups stockpiling heavy weapons and ammunition in these mountains for months. One only had to look as far as the wounded ANA and ANP soldiers being carried on stretchers onto the Blackhawk helicopters to see the obvious truth of these claims.

Shortly, CAS was confirmed to be available to us, provided that we could meet the rules-of-engagement conditions that I will explain shortly. With such a large target, we would likely get a B-1 bomber for an initial series of bombing runs, followed by Apache helicopters to clean up any remaining enemy who managed to survive the initial pounding.

Now, a quick note about the rules of engagement for using close air support. Before any CAS package could be sent to us to unleash armament on the enemy forces, a technical rule had to be satisfied. In order for us to use CAS, we had to have "eyes on" our target. In other words, an American soldier had to be able to tell the bomber on the radio, "Yes, the bad guys are at grid XYZ, I see them, bombs away." But at this moment in time, all friendly forces had pulled back from the base of the mountain to this command post approximately five kilometers from the enemy positions. No one, Afghan or American, had eyes on the enemy.

Knowing that any movement by our small and outnumbered force to put eyes on the enemy would only result in more friendly wounded or killed, I did my best to try and find a middle-ground solution. Perhaps an Apache helicopter could do a low-altitude nape-of-earth flyby, and either visually confirm the enemy locations, which would satisfy the requirement for American eyes on, or even better, the Apache could engage the Taliban directly. This alternative plan was not approved.

So we watched the sun slowly setting while levels of command well above Captain Cain and myself debated this problem intensely. What appeared to be a pointless bureaucratic rule was the only thing standing between killing hundreds of Taliban and letting them escape.

Thank God for pointless bureaucratic rules. In the minutes while this wrangling was occurring, a handsome, well-dressed man in his early forties with a striking black beard approached Captain Cain. With his equally well-dressed and well-armed entourage, he introduced himself as a member of the Afghan National Parliament.

He explained in a calm and relaxed voice that he was a member of the Cuchie caucus in parliament, and that he had received a desperate cell phone call from a Cuchie elder directly involved in the conflict. With a serious face, he offered a startling revelation for all the military and police personnel present: "There are no Taliban on that mountain. They are Cuchie civilians."

While Captain Cain was having this conversation about twenty meters away from me, I was still by the Humvee, on the radio, and in the final phases of executing a compromise solution to the problem of having no eyes on the enemy positions. Higher-ups had agreed it was not wise to "endanger the brave men on the ground with a high-risk reconnaissance on the mountain." So they wanted us to at least get close enough that we could warn the bomber if we saw any civilians moving in the area, but remain out of range of the enemy's powerful Dyshka machine gun. If we could do this, the bomber would then make a pass at the mountain.

Finally a carefully negotiated plan was in place to deal a deathblow to this huge Taliban force. I was tweaking with the excitement and power of playing God with the lives of hundreds of enemy combatants. For months we had been getting ambushed by Taliban and losing good men in combat. Now I had the chance to really hit the Taliban hard. It goes without saying that when Captain Cain told me to stop everything and put CAS on hold, I was dumbfounded.

Instead of sending our military recon force down toward the valley and the occupied mountain, the Cuchie member of parliament, with his entourage in tow, climbed into a dusty but new Toyota Land Cruiser and headed off in that same direction. Everyone else, so close to an orgy of destruction, scratched their heads at the strange turn of events. Instead of the excitement of watching a battalion of Taliban be obliterated, we settled in for a cold, tedious, and sleepless night, awaiting the return of this Cuchie politician.

The sun eventually rose. Not another bullet was fired, nor were any bombs dropped from any aircraft. My innocent and unsuspecting attempts at bombing the mountain were thwarted, and as a result (thankfully) there was no Afghan My Lai Massacre by the Garden of Eden. The Cuchie politician proved himself to be a sophisticated deal maker. He managed to get both sides to agree to negotiations. Hostages were released that same day and compensation for the slain child and the confiscated livestock was arranged. Neither group in this remote area had a newfound outpouring of love for the other, but they had settled the issue with honor.

As we drove out of the small village center, and slowly climbed up the small hill heading home, the Garden of Eden again came into view. But like the mythological Garden of Eden, spoiled by Eve's selfish indiscretion, this small green paradise had also become tainted by spilled blood. Instead of a curious woman, this paradise had been ruined by the thirst of a horse. We made the turn by the large rock outcropping, and the green space disappeared from my view forever.

OPERATION IRON RAGE

The maneuver forces from Provincial Reconstruction Team Ghazni were made up predominantly from the 102nd Infantry Battalion, 29th Division, and went by the moniker Iron Grays. They brought a lot of iron and steel to the fight and had the tendency to use "Iron" in the code name for their missions, as was the case with Operation Iron Rage, a sub-operation of Operation Mountain Fury. Operation Iron Rage involved the might of one company of 10th Mountain Infantry, the 102nd, and our ETTs and ANA.

This operation involved a lot of moving parts and pieces, and was designed to catch two cells of Taliban that had been operating in Qarabagh district, approximately forty kilometers south of our FOB in Ghazni. Coalition Forces were air assaulted into the mountains behind where we expected to find the enemy. Our ETT forces traveled by ground to encircle suspected enemy positions and deny them a route of escape.

As the OIC (officer in charge) of the ANA-ETT forces deployed, my focus was on what we called a screen, a mobile moving cordon that aimed to locate, capture, or kill any enemy who attempted to escape from the air-assaulted troops pushing them out of the mountains.

During the whole of Operation Iron Rage, involving hundreds of combined friendly forces over five days, only one small group of eight soldiers actually came into contact with the enemy.

And through a series of events that can only be explained through *inshallah*, it should be no surprise that this group of eight soldiers was comprised of myself, CPT Komar, and a handful of ANA soldiers. Furthermore, when this engagement unfolded, we were outnumbered two to one, isolated, with no radio communication, and exposed on an open mountainside, while the enemy was well dug in and defended.

In the weeks following these events, my ETT teammate Sergeant First Class Bernard Deghand would face an almost identical situation, and would end up being carried off the mountain dead. He was a man more experienced and tenacious in leading soldiers than I could ever hope to be, but I walked away from my mountain engagement completely victorious and with no injuries to any friendly forces. *Inshallah*.

During a village patrol earlier that day, we were told by pro-government villagers that the enemy had been using a certain mountain as a nightly base camp. The mountain was named Tand Ghar. As it was midday, I assumed (incorrectly) that the camp would be unoccupied. So with minimal forces, we began our climb up the mountain. I, a fellow ETT, and about six ANA soldiers slowly made the arduous ascent. The rest of the ANA company were supposed to join us, but seemed to stall out about halfway up the hill.

So in a relaxed posture, our small squad-sized group

continued our slow climb. Being bogged down with body armor and other equipment, I fell to the back of the group with my ETT partner, Captain Komar. The unencumbered ANA quickly passed us, and made it to the ridgeline first. Within seconds, their AK-47s were firing en masse.

I stood there in disbelief, gasping for air from the strenuous climb and the high altitude. At this moment I realized my lackadaisical approach to this mountain had allowed me to forget to grab my handheld radio.

Crap.

With an extra rush of adrenaline, I pushed up over the ridge to catch up with and support the small number of ANA soldiers who were already in action. As I ran across the flat mountaintop, I took note of a well-developed Taliban camp. It had an extensive maze of rock fighting positions, a meeting area, and a sleeping area filled with blankets and mats. By this time the ANA had assaulted forward, cleared the enemy from the top of the ridge, and were in hot pursuit. The enemy was in full retreat down the other side of the mountain. I stood there in amazement that this larger force had decided to flee when they could have easily wiped us all out in the open while we climbed. Perhaps the large number of ANA soldiers remaining at the bottom of the other side of the mountain had prompted their retreat. Had they engaged us, they would have all died on that mountaintop, because our air and artillery would have eventually destroyed them in place. They chose to flee and fight another day.

As I watched the ant-sized enemy soldiers scattering into the valley below, out of our small-weapons range, I began to hear the heavy, sustained staccato of machine-gun fire. Not knowing who was firing or at whom, I dove behind a big rock, injuring my leg in the process. Come to find out, it was ANA soldiers firing at us. The remaining ANA force left at the base of the mountain had wheeled around to the south, and could not decide whether the silhouettes they saw on the ridge were friend or foe, so they decided to shoot anyway. At least one hundred rounds were aimed at us by the ANA, who mistook us for Taliban. With no radio, I was unable to relay to my ETT soldiers down below to tell the ANA to cease fire. Fortunately, none of us were hit, but suffice to say that in my whole yearlong tour, this moment was when I had the most bullets shot at me. All of which came from "friendly" weapons.

Once the confusion was cleared up, we safely descended the mountain and rejoined the rest of my ANA-ETT element. We requested an artillery barrage from the 102nd Battalion to destroy the Taliban mountain camp, and it came in with pinpoint accuracy.

Tand Ghar Mountain, with smoke from the artillery round explosions landing on the Taliban camp that was located along its ridgeline.

LAUGHTER IS OUR

BEST DEFENSE

TRAINING FOR IRAQ

Despite the unique and important counterinsurgency role of the ETT, the training we received for the mission erroneously prepared us for a traditional Army war in traditional Army ways. We spent three months brushing up our conventional warrior skills at Camp Shelby, Mississippi, with only a couple days' worth of relevant counterinsurgency training. As perhaps the best example of wasted opportunity at Camp Shelby, more time was spent on the proper wear and use of nuclear/chemical/biological gear and personal decontamination than was spent on learning the culture and history of Afghanistan. (FYI: The first thing you do when you get to Afghanistan is put your nuclear/biological/chemical suit into storage, because there is no enemy threat capability in this area.)

Another clue that things had gone off course during our train-up at Camp Shelby was the fact that our instructors regularly told us what to expect in Iraq. Aside from the fact that this wasn't the country we were deploying to, it was also like comparing apples to hand grenades. Iraq, an Arab country, modern and educated, with natural resources to support its economy, has little to no similarity to Persian Afghanistan, broken and trapped in the poverty of the Stone Age. Perhaps the only commonality between the two countries was that both are the victims of poorly managed counterinsurgency campaigns by the U.S. military and civilian leadership, despite the heroic efforts of American soldiers fighting there.

Whenever Iraq was mentioned, we would immediately interrupt our instructors and remind them that we were ETTs, and we were going to "the other war." To a man, they would reply with this infamous quote: "Well . . . I don't know how they do it in Afghanistan, but this is how we do it in Iraq."

In the end, the train-up and preparation were ill-suited for the yearlong embedding into the chaos and dysfunction that is life inside the ANA. By the time the scope of our three-month training disaster was fully realized by most of us, it was too late. We were off to a yearlong tour in Afghanistan, experts at using our nuclear/chemical/biological suits, but clueless as to the language, culture, and history of the Afghan people.

When we arrived in country after a twenty-four-hour flight, we got a three-day brush-up on Big Army's training, with further briefings on being risk-averse, putting safety first, and most important, pumped with new warnings not to trust, nor get too close to, our Afghan Army counterparts. Finally we were herded onto a Chinook helicopter, broken up into small groups of one, two, or three, and unceremoniously whisked off to our new homes: desolate and remote ANA Forward Operating Bases, where for the most part we were to spend the year undersupplied, under-supported, and overly criticized by our U.S. Army Headquarters for "going native."

Camp Phoenix, Kabul: My group of New York Army National Guard ETTs from the Twenty-seventh Brigade Combat Team, newly arrived in country, preparing to load onto Chinooks for transport to our ANA FOBs in the eastern part of Afghanistan.

Here on the ANA bases, we gave up the safety and pre-dictability of going to war with large, organized American Army units and accepted the fact that our fate was in the hands of the ANA (the same people we were warned not to trust). Luckily for us, we had our nuclear/chemical/biolog-ical suits to protect us, and a lot of Iraq-centered training to carry us through the year.

THE RANGE

arget practice is a relatively easy task for a group of soldiers to accomplish. It requires a remote and unpopulated area in which to shoot, paper targets, and wooden target stands. In America it would take a few dollars, a quick trip to a hardware store, and a couple of hours to build the latter.

Things take a little longer in Afghanistan. We were tasked with conducting a weapons qualification training event for Afghan soldiers, but executing this simple mission took weeks.

First off, we didn't have a Home Depot out in rural Afghanistan, so building the wooden target stands had to be contracted out to an Afghan carpenter. At our base a whitebearded elder we called "the Godfather" controlled all such contracts through a mix of threats and patronage, price gouging and delaying any project to ensure his desired level of graft. Then there was the issue of quality control. We drew up plans for the wooden target stands and gave them to the carpenter who the Godfather had selected for the job.

But when the stands arrived, they had not been built to the needed specifications. More days passed before the proper frames were built and delivered. The final price for the wooden stands was so inflated it would have made an American defense contractor envious.

Another obstacle was the Afghan soldiers themselves. They had a strong dislike of training of any type, and the idea of target practice left them unimpressed. We would schedule a date for the weapons qualification, and they would cancel it. The excuses for the cancellation varied: it was too cold, or there was not enough fuel in the vehicles to get them to the range location. My favorite was when the Afghan supply sergeant informed us that all the ammo was locked up, and the officer with the key was on vacation for two weeks. This really caught our attention, because we were living in a war zone, where the ability to have extra ammunition handy is about as important as having oxygen to breathe.

In time we came up with a way to get the Afghan soldiers to show up for training events. We bribed their leadership with odds and ends like printer cartridges, pens, and dry-erase boards, which they would receive if they delivered their soldiers.

After weeks of waiting for the stars to align, all the ingredients were in place and we conducted our weapons qualification. But as the first groups of soldiers completed their firing, the paper targets revealed very few hits. Shooting tips were given, and weapons were resighted, but this failed to improve results. So with limited daylight remaining, our group of American advisors decided to do the only thing left to improve scores. We moved the targets closer to the shooters. When this produced the same inadequate results, we moved the target stands even closer.

The poor results were enough to convince the Afghans that they needed more weapons practice, and seeing as we already had the target stands built, future weapons qualifications would be easier to conduct. That is, until someone came up with the bright idea to shoot higher-caliber weapons at the targets. Within minutes, machine guns and rocket-propelled grenades were blazing away, and when the smoke cleared, our overpriced wooden target frames had been reduced to smoking splinters.

To complete this comedy of errors, it was only then, when we began packing up to leave our firing range, that anyone noticed the funny little red-painted stones that were peeking through what remained of the light snow that blanketed the ground. We had picked the site for our range because it was close to our base, and because it was in an area that was unlikely to be attacked by the Taliban. When we did our reconnaissance on it, the layer of snow had obscured the fact that the area had been marked as a minefield.

It was a miracle that no one stepped on a mine, as we had over one hundred soldiers on the range. Suffice to say that as we left the area, we laughed out loud at our silly mistake and good fortune.

This Weapons Qualification Range experience was a pretty good metaphor for the war as a whole: lots of time and planning to accomplish a mission without fully achieving the desired results; an over-expenditure of resources and, ultimately, a loss of investment; exposure to unknown and unpredicted dangers and the luck to survive them.

SELF-PRESERVATION VS. COMBAT STREET CRED

A mortar round makes a unique sound when it explodes.

If I had to spell it out, it would look like this: "KRUNK."

It's nothing like the explosions of bombs in Hollywood movies.

And today, while enjoying a relaxed afternoon in surprisingly warm and sunny weather (it's been cold and wet lately), our ears heard this distinctive "KRUNK" violently break the silence outside our FOB.

The immediate reaction to hearing any explosion is denial. For a split second, your brain hopes it didn't really hear that noise, and you try your hardest to pretend it wasn't really there. Noises like "KRUNK" rarely bring enjoyable moments of peace and relaxation. But once this delusional pretending game runs its course, the next response is to accept reality and respond to it. In this case, the proper response would be to throw yourself on the ground and yell, "Oh shit, that's a MORTAR!"

Now that would be the proper and logical thing to do, but here is where it gets tricky. We have to factor in a variable I'll call "combat street cred." Seeing as we are guys, and being guys who are performing in a testosterone-saturated environment, one's response to a potentially life-threatening noise is to be torn between self-preservation and the equally important preservation of combat street cred. The self-preservation part of your mind tells you to dive into the mud, and low crawl over to your body armor and helmet.

But the street cred part of your brain says, "Never let them see you sweat!" It tells you to stand there, looking unimpressed, and not bothered by the inconvenience of a violent death.

When the first mortar round landed, I was sitting in my chair, instant messaging a close friend back home online. The door to our room was open, and I had a view of my ETT comrades sitting outside in the sunlight.

I instant messaged my friend, "I think we are getting mortared."

She replied, "Oh My God! Do you need to go?"

I wrote, "No, not yet."

I heard my buddies right outside the door go silent after they all heard the first "KRUNK." Then, as if on cue, their combined military experiences came flowing out of their mouths like verbal diarrhea. They were cold-blooded pros at the combat street cred game.

"One-twenties—big mortar tubes!" shouted Looney.

"Hope that's friendly fire!" said Glidden.

"Is the PRT [U.S. base] firing? Is it the fucking PRT?" shouted another.

"H.E., baby! High explosive!" said Looney.

Then silence. No one would crack and run for cover. No one was blinking. It was a game of chicken with possibly deadly consequences. The only guy to move was Staff Sergeant Glidden, who ran past me in the doorway to check our "FOB ATTACK POOL" board we had hanging on our wall. For ten bucks, each ETT got to pick his guess of what date our FOB will get attacked next. Much like a "Hollywood Death Pool," it was a morbid stab at humor. Apparently, Glidden wanted to see if he was going to win the pot of money if this was indeed an attack.

Then another KRUNK.

And another. And another.

And fortunately for us, they were not moving closer, which meant they were not enemy rounds being adjusted onto our FOB. They were in fact the Eighty-second Airborne, registering their mortars from their positions on their U.S. base a few miles away from our ANA FOB.

I exhaled in relief, and refocused on my emails and instant messages. My buddies continued their interrupted war stories with a new focus on those that had something to do with mortar attacks.

OF "POO" AND POP-TARTS

POO is one of many new Army acronyms that pepper the vocabulary here in Afghanistan. And today, Ski, Vandy, and I, along with a platoon of ANA, got tasked with a mission to go find us some POO.

The acronym stands for "Point of Origin," and applies specifically to the location where rockets or mortars are launched. On this sunny day, we were told to find the POO for a handful of 107mm rockets that had been launched by the Taliban into downtown Ghazni City. The early-morning rockets had landed and exploded in the civilian center of the city, and had hit civilian homes and shops. It was a reckless and wanton attack that hit innocent civilians as they began their day cooking breakfasts for their children and families.

Normally, these searches for POO sites are wild-goose chases into the hinterlands. Based on crater analysis of where the rocket exploded, we can estimate a distance and direction of where the rockets came from. "Estimate" is the key word here, as this is not an exact science. Actually finding a POO site requires more luck than skill, and more often than not, the POO site remains undiscovered after hours of searching.

But when the Taliban's rockets are flying, and a mission comes down from higher to find where they are launching them from, we don't get much choice in the matter. So armed with the limited info we can glean from the crater, Ski, Vandy, and I, accompanied by ANA, led a mission to go find the POO site for this rocket attack this morning. At best, we could find and kill the Taliban launching them, or locate their cache of rockets, and at the least, we could mark the location for further surveillance operations.

We aimed our Humvee toward our estimated POO grid location and headed out west into an area we had never visited before. Unfortunately, there are no straight roads in Ghazni, so we took a long, circuitous route that zigzagged through villages, mountains, and dried-up riverbeds. While passing through one shallow, dry riverbed, Ski and I fell victim to the classic mental escapism that plagues wild-goose-chase missions like this. Ski was driving, and I was jabbering away about God knows what, when Vandy unexpectedly screamed from the gun turret, "STOP!" Ski slammed on the brakes. I slammed into the windshield, and Vandy slammed into the butt stock of the M240 Bravo machine gun.

Once we recovered from the initial surprise of the abrupt stop, Vandy calmly told Ski to back up slowly. After a few seconds, the cause of Vandy's scream became visible. In the middle of the road, sticking up like a tombstone in front of our Humvee, was the large tail fin of a mortar round partially buried in the crusty riverbed. Next to the tail fin was recently disturbed earth. The two together were the hallmark of an IED.

I ordered Ski to back up a good seventy-five meters, and then had Latif, our interpreter, tell the ANA to dismount from their pickup trucks, which were following behind us, and pull security on the hilltops surrounding the riverbed. Explicit instructions were given to stay at least seventy-five meters away from the mortar round IED. Ski and I then pulled out a map and started focusing in on finding our grid location, so we could get an EOD (Explosive Ordnance Disposal) team to come and disarm this potential IED.

While we huddled over the map on the hood of the Humvee, I heard the crunching of rocks and dirt behind me, and looked over my shoulder to see two ANA soldiers walking toward us. One of the soldiers was haphazardly holding the mortar round in hand. Despite our clear instructions to stay clear of it, these two soldiers had decided to single-handedly yank it out of the ground to speed things along. They didn't feel like sitting around for hours waiting for an EOD team to show up, and took it upon themselves to resolve the standoff.

Luckily for them, the mortar round was a rusted-out dud that had been partially buried in this riverbed since the Russian invasion. The disturbed earth next to it, according to the ANA, had nothing to do with the mortar round, but was instead a sign that goats had been nosing around for water in that spot earlier in the day.

The good news was there was no IED, and none of us were in any danger. But to brazenly tempt fate and yank it out of the ground was a risk only the two Afghan soldiers seemed willing to take. While their approach to this problem was reckless and borderline suicidal, in the end it proved to be the decision that saved us hours of waiting for EOD, and allowed us to continue on our mission of finding the POO site.

After we left the riverbed, we spent the next couple hours driving aimlessly from village to village, asking anyone we could find if they knew where the POO site was. We must have talked to more than fifty people, but it should be no surprise that no one had any worthwhile info to share. They all said they heard rockets flying overhead earlier in the day, but didn't know who had launched them or where they had launched them from. We were ready to write the day off as a classic wild-goose chase.

It was getting late, and my sixth sense was starting to get spooked, so I decided we would hit one more village and then head back. Our POO hunting patrol was small in size, and I felt we were very vulnerable to a complex ambush. It was a known fact there were Taliban in the area, as they had launched rockets earlier in the day from this general vicinity.

As we drove up to the final village that I had selected for questioning, I told Ski to park on the outskirts of town, and let the ANA dismount and go talk to the villagers themselves. I already knew we wouldn't get any help from the villagers, as no one in this area seemed too interested in helping out Americans.

I sat in the passenger seat, with the door open, snacking on some blueberry Pop-Tarts. Pop-Tarts are in ample supply in Afghanistan, and every chow hall has boxes and boxes of them sitting ready to be looted by hungry soldiers. We regularly loaded up our Humvee with snacks such as this, as we never knew if we would be stranded out on mission and in need of food.

So as I munched away on Pop-Tarts, enjoying the nice weather, Afghan children congregated around our Humvee in hopes of getting a free pen or a piece of candy. The ANA eventually returned from the village, empty-handed and with no new information about the POO. I chalked up the day as another waste of time and resources in our fight against the Taliban, and we began to pack up our stuff to return home to FOB Ghazni.

As I picked up an empty Skoal dip can and water bottles that we had inadvertently strewn around the ground, I noticed an unopened packet of blueberry Pop-Tarts still sitting on the hood of the Humvee. I grabbed it, and on a whim, asked Latif to tell the Afghan kids who were still milling around that I would give the packet of Pop-Tarts to the first kid to tell me where the rockets came from.

Almost immediately after Latif delivered this message

The secret weapon for getting information from Afghans: Pop-Tarts!

to the children assembled around the Humvee, one young boy pointed to a small, rocky hill no more than five hundred meters to our west. He chattered away to Latif, who turned to me and said, "The boy says he saw men launch the rockets on the side of that hill this morning. He wants his Pop-Tarts now."

Sure enough, with our trusty pair of binoculars we could see on the very hill the child pointed to the blackened patches of rock and sand that were burned by the propellant of the 107mm rockets as they began their flight toward downtown Ghazni.

The lesson I learned on this day was simple. Elders are cautious, and are more susceptible to the threats of the Taliban. They don't want to share information with us, even if they support the ANA and the Coalition Forces, because they don't want to face reprisals when the Taliban returns later in the day after we have returned to our safe FOB. However, children are simpler, and don't fully understand the complex pressures being exerted by the Taliban. They will reveal things that elders will hide.

So the lesson learned is simple: Don't ignore the kids. Always ask them what's going on. And always pack lots of Pop-Tarts!

THIS NICKNAME HAS A NICE RING TO IT

There are three guarantees in Army life—age-old, time-tested truisms. If you ask any veteran anywhere, regardless of the war or unit they served in, they will nod their heads in agreement. The three givens are:

1. Your unit will have some guy with a hard-to-pronounce, multisyllabic Eastern European last name. Usually Polish.
2. Your unit will have a guy from Texas.
3. You will get a nickname.

These were all proven to be true in my experience at war. Corporal Radek Polanski gave us the hard-to-pronounce name. We also had a guy from Texas on our ETT team who, in a classic cowboy drawl, spent as much time telling us about mules and chuck wagons and rodeos as he did talking Army business. And I got a nickname. A military nickname is normally forged through some act performed in the line of duty. Rarely is this act complimentary or positive. Usually the nickname is a result of misfortune, an accident, or an act of sheer stupidity.

Three of my ETT teammates provide a range of examples of how the nickname process works. One has a record of inadvertently breaking equipment and has consistently been able to make communications equipment inoperable, so he is known as Dark Cloud. Another officer, blessed with an incredible intellect but cursed with a physically large head, is known as Mardi Gras Head (think of the big-headed parade floats in New Orleans). Last, an operations officer got the deserved and very unfunny nickname of Deathwish for his incredible ability to make horrible tactical decisions at the worst possible moments, while regularly sending us out on missions without adequate planning, preparation, or personnel.

Nicknames are like throwing spaghetti at the wall; it may take a few tries before one sticks. I've had a few thrown at me that didn't. These included Captain Prozac and Captain Barbiturate, in reference to the post-traumatic stress disorder (PTSD) sleep and antidepressant medications I'd been prescribed by Army medical staff. I also was given Captain Care Bear for the humanitarian aid project I started, which collected stuffed animals and winter clothing for hundreds of children in our area of operations.

None of these were as creative, humorous, or appropriately disturbing as the lasting nickname I eventually received from my teammates. It's short and simple, sounds good on the surface, and captures both humor and misfortune.

Ring.

Short for *ringworm*.

Back in the fall, while out on a combat mission, I got a gash on my leg, and somehow this pesky fungal infection took root. When I told some of my buddies what the strange

Captain Tupper, a.k.a. Captain Care Bear, loaded up with toys for a humanitarian aid mission with the Blackfoot ETTs.

scabby circle on my leg was, they all recoiled in disgust, and it wasn't too long until I was greeted by teammates with the new nickname. Ring is a classic military nickname with a classic repulsive story to go with it. The infection is now long gone. The nickname will likely last a lifetime.

THE "MONKEY AND THE TYPEWRITER" ALLEGORY

Have you heard the allegory of the "Monkey and the Typewriter"? The premise is that if you give a monkey a typewriter and an eternity of time, he will eventually write a best seller. Well, that's what it feels like here: we are the monkeys who bang away on the keyboard, trying to produce something worth the effort. We seem to have a lot of time and we make many attempts to accomplish tactical successes with the missions we run. Yet unfortunately, we seem to come up empty most of the time. Suffice to say, it feels like we are monkeys aimlessly producing nothing of value.

But eventually, as suggested by the allegory, the monkey streams together a string of random keystrokes and produces something worthy of publishing. That is what occurred today: a successful tactical result, totally unplanned and unpredicted.

One of the gripes we as ETTs have is that our ANA soldiers have a knack for wandering off post to pursue the civilian creature comforts, such as going to the marketplaces or restaurants, or visiting friends (possibly even a clandestine love interest).

Who knows what the reason they sneak off base is, we just know that at any given point in time some of our Afghan soldiers have "escaped" and are out doing some shopping.

And today was no different. A couple of our Afghan soldiers found themselves enjoying lunch at a local restaurant, which was an unauthorized journey, to say the least. As luck would have it, at the same time a couple of Taliban/al-Qaeda types had decided to spend their afternoon planting some disguised explosive devices at a major traffic intersection between the marketplace and our FOB entrance. The timing devices on the bombs went off early, and exploded right after they placed them in the intersection.

Enter the ANA soldiers filling their stomachs at the restaurant. Apparently these terrorists didn't realize that they were within feet of the ANA, who summarily dropped their forks and picked up their rifles, and commenced chasing and shooting the stunned and fleeing terrorists.

On this day, the proverbial monkey author typed up a grand short story, which ended with terrorists in custody, some with gunshot wounds, and no civilian injuries from their premature bomb blasts. One can only hope this monkey writes a sequel, because storybook endings like this are few and far between here in eastern Afghanistan.

HOW TO WIN THE WAR

Billions of dollars have been spent in an attempt to defeat the Taliban and their fundamentalist foreign fighter allies. Hundreds of Coalition soldiers and thousands of Afghans have lost their lives fighting, a cost that cannot be measured. Yet despite these efforts, the situation seems to be getting worse, not better.

I've given this issue lots of thought, and I've come up with a guaranteed solution for peace, stability, and victory against intolerance and fundamentalism in Afghanistan.

History has shown us that the military approach has never worked. For hundreds of years, no one has successfully occupied this country. The mighty British Empire fought three wars here (not including their current efforts in Kandahar), and lost every time. The full weight of the Soviet military got bogged down and whipped in an unsuccessful ten-year war. After the Russians finally left, even the Afghans, during what is referred to as the Kabul Civil Wars, couldn't defeat each other. So why should the United States and its Coalition partners expect to fare any better?

I've come to reject the notion that this war can be won solely through military means. We need to think outside of the box.

It is my conclusion, based on the pseudoscientific research I've conducted on myself during months of female deprivation, that the root of all Afghan problems resides in the pent-up desires and frustrations of Afghan men. They are denied any access to women until marriage, and even then it's a hit-or-miss commitment to a woman they've probably never made eye contact with. The men are frustrated, *sexually frustrated*, to the point that they pick up guns, put on their finest suicide vests, and get their energy out through holy war. It's the only rational explanation for the macho warrior culture of Afghanistan, and if you take the Koran at its word, it's the quickest way to meet girls and land a lot of virgins. If you were denied any contact (personal, social, sexual) with women until your wedding day, *wouldn't you want to kill someone?*

No matter what group of men you asked this of, the chorus of "*Yes!*" would be deafening.

So here is my master plan: Let's import fifty thousand Brazilian women and one thousand Italian-American women into Afghanistan.

Seriously.

If you unleash this untamed and passionate assault wave of female sexuality onto this country, it won't be long until Afghan women are streaming to the spa to get a Brazilian wax. Burning burkhas will illuminate the streets as women march to purchase thong bikinis. Within weeks, the sounds of the "Lambada" and "The Girl from Ipanema" will replace IED blasts and gunfire.

The Italian-American girls, in addition to their good looks, will add the dominating leadership and personal for-

titude needed to bring this revolution to its successful finish. They will act as the enforcers of this sexual revolution,
making sure the Brazilians stay mission-focused. These
olive-skinned beauties will be in charge of beating the hard-
core male resisters with their fiery personalities. If that fails,
they will just use their beautiful almond-colored eyes to
stare down the men, with that infamous expression anyone
married to an Italian girl knows all too well: "Oh no, you
didn't just go there." Taliban will cower and beg forgiveness, and this war will be over before you can say "*Ciao,
bella.*"

Anyone with a better idea, speak up.

FOBBITS PART 1: AN INTRODUCTION

Not all soldiers face the risks and hardships of front-line combatants. It is a little-known fact that the down-range trigger-pullers are a minority among the soldiers in Afghanistan. The majority live a much more accommodating and safe lifestyle.

Have you heard of the Fobbit? It's the nickname for this second, larger group of soldiers. A lot of people don't realize it, but for every fighting soldier there are eight to eleven soldiers who serve in logistical and support roles—medics, truck drivers, mail handlers, fuelers, military police—and rarely have contact with enemy forces. While the trigger-pullers go out on missions daily to root out the enemy, these support soldiers spend most of their time in relative safety on the well-protected and -defended FOBs. Thus, with a nod to the most well-fed denizens of Middle Earth, the term Fobbits.

Fobbits have it easy, what with little to no exposure to the enemy, plus all the creature comforts of the FOB—from massages to pedicures to smoothies to 24-7 coffee shops and deluxe chow halls.

The animosity between the two groups is in part good-natured ribbing, but there is real resentment of the easy living enjoyed by the Fobbits, while we are downrange in life-or-death situations. This resentment is fueled by the fact that there is no difference between the pay and benefits of a Fobbit and a frontline trigger-puller. The desk clerk who eats at Burger King each day and goes to the movie theater each night at one of the larger FOBs gets the same hazard and combat pay that I receive. And I haven't seen a Whopper or movie in months!

In the spirit of full disclosure, there is one benefit that the Fobbits can't earn. And that is the honor and prestige of being in the worst places, at the worst times, and doing the most difficult job in the world. One of the most respected awards you can get in the military is the CIB, the Combat Infantryman Badge. This badge shows all that you have been in combat and that you lived to tell the tale. While the

Bagram Air Base: Home of the Whopper, Fobbits, and Dairy Queen.

Army has recently created the Combat Action Badge (CAB) for all non-infantry soldiers who have been in combat, regardless of their duty position or training, it remains the redheaded stepchild of the CIB.

The truth is, despite the grumblings and tirades about Fobbits, very few frontline combatants would voluntarily change places for safer jobs in the rear. The honor and respect earned in performing daily combat operations far outweigh the enjoyment of Whoppers and movies.

FOBBITS PART 2: CREATURE COMFORTS

The nickname "Fobbit" sounds cute and fuzzy, but it's not meant to be. Many a fistfight in Afghanistan and Iraq has started with the insult "Fobbit" being levied by one soldier toward another.

In late July, I found myself trapped in Fobbit nirvana for over two weeks, awaiting medical tests related to dizzy spells and an irregular heartbeat. Bagram Air Force Base is a huge built-up military metropolis with thousands of inhabitants. It's got a Burger King, pizza shop, Popeyes, continuing education center, salsa dance classes, a twenty-four-hour chow hall (with an average of about fifty meal selections each day, all of which are high-class and tasty). It has all sorts of stores, and even a beauty salon offering pedicures, manicures, and massages. It's like a real American city, except almost everyone is in some sort of military uniform.

Bagram also has something extra-special for your average horny infantryman: *Women!* There are lots of women: Chinese women, Russian women, American women, Australian, British, and Eastern European women, and even Afghan women (sans burkha). Most, with the exception of the Afghan women, are bebopping around in shorts and skimpy T-shirts. The scenery is deluxe!

And it should go without saying that Bagram, given these conditions of leisure and eye candy, is the utopian homeland for Fobbits. Many if not most of the people stationed there have no concept of life "outside the wire." Their tour of Afghanistan is one in which they will never hear a shot fired, never go without three square meals a day, and never want for a hot shower.

Fobbits are annoying reminders of the unequal risk distribution in Army life. The Bagram Fobbits are a finger-in-the-eye reminder that while you're sweating and eating dust and dodging lead, some of your brothers and sisters in arms are at Burger King, enjoying your rightful Whopper-sized share of the easy life.

Bagram Air Base: Fobbits enjoy a broad selection of high-quality foods at this large chow hall.

FOBBITS PART 3: MANUFACTURING DANGER

I spent two weeks in Bagram waiting for medical testing, stuck in the land of the Whopper until the Bagram Medical Unit received a resupply of the materials needed to conduct the tests. Once I got this completed, I was free to return to my little corner of hell down in Ghazni, where the term "flame-broiled" has a totally different meaning.

During these two weeks, I didn't acquire any new exciting or depressing war stories to pass along, as there is no war to speak of in Fobbit nirvana. Absent any real threat, the powers that be at Bagram have dug up some B-list threats, and have established some ridiculous safety policies with the intent to keep us all on our toes.

First, and one of my favorites, is the safety belt policy. The Army-issued safety belt, also known as the reflective belt, is a traffic-yellow belt (orange, blue, or pink are also available, to suit your fashion taste) that is worn around the waist. The policy here requires that the belt must be worn, and it's funny as hell to see strapping soldiers in their ACUs (the new digital camouflage uniform pattern) wearing a

Day-Glo sash as they wander around post conducting their business. It brings out a *Queer Eye for the Straight Guy* aspect of our uniform that was sorely lacking.

Another policy that seems out of place is that all soldiers at all times must carry one weapon anywhere they go—to the latrine, to eat, to watch a movie, even to the Bagram-sponsored salsa dance lessons. This carry policy is normal for us out on the front lines, but here at Bagram the only shots fired are suicides or those discharged by accident. It would probably be safer to leave all the weapons locked up.

Soldiers in direct combat capacities are issued M4 carbines (a shorter version of the M16, with a collapsible stock) and M9 pistols (Berettas). We are accustomed to carrying a weapon (or two) wherever we go. But the rear-echelon soldiers, a.k.a. Fobbits, are issued the old-school M16, which is a long rifle. Carrying this thing around is like having a third leg, and if you're short, it's like dragging a small tree around with you. Seeing someone with this longer weapon is one of the easiest and fastest ways to identify a Fobbit. On Bagram, an M16 is more likely to have pizza grease on it than gun grease.

The final example of Bagram's "manufactured danger" is its speed limits. Of course, limiting speed is a prudent and wise decision for the base commanders. But here in Camp Lacey (the medical unit's camp within Bagram Air Force Base, where I currently reside) the posted speed limit is three mph.

Three mph!

Where did they get this number from? Was four mph already taken? Was five mph deemed too reckless and unsafe a speed? Ten mph was obviously out of the question—the crumpled and flattened bodies would be lining the streets if vehicles traveled at ten mph.

Hell, at three mph people should just get out and walk—they would arrive at their destination faster.

So you can see that the military culture is constantly looking for a threat, real or perceived. Or in this case, real or manufactured. I'd recommend to the base commanders that if they want to deal with a real threat, they should close Burger King. Do they have any idea what that food does to your cholesterol level? Heart attacks have killed more soldiers on Bagram than vehicles going ten mph.

MISSING IN ACTION: JACK, BUD, AND JIM

I've mentioned the dearth of women in Afghanistan, with the exception of Bagram, where they seem to grow on trees. But there is another essential ingredient to a soldier's life that is AWOL here, and that is alcohol.

Jack, Bud, and Jim are not the first names of missing combatants lost in hard-fought battles. They are the preferred alcoholic beverages of the U.S. soldier: Jack Daniel's, Budweiser, and Jim Beam. And boy, are they missed!

The Army is not an alcoholic and does not need these lubricants in order to perform. All alcohol is prohibited for all U.S. personnel in Afghanistan, and despite this prohibition, we are performing our mission quite well. Most soldiers will go a year without the nectar of the gods. I say most because not all is dry here. There are ways and means to get drunk, and some American soldiers risk serious punishments to get their groove on. Some of our European allies are permitted to drink, and the French and Romanian soldiers have regular beer and wine happy hours that tease the thirsts of Americans, who can only sit back and watch.

Afghans also sell alcohol, but it's hidden behind shelves in most of the bazaars in the country. And it's not homemade moonshine we are talking about—it's the good stuff. Jack and Jim are here, you just have to know who to ask to find them.

The best way to acquire a bottle of whiskey or a six-pack of beer is to use an Afghan as the middleman. For most soldiers, this middleman is the Terp, more formally known as the combat interpreter. As ETTs, we each have our own personal Terp at our disposal, so if the mood strikes, and you're really thirsty, your Terp can hook you up lickety-split.

The bad news is that a bottle of Jack can set you back $70 U.S. And that's just for regular Old No. 7 Jack Daniel's. We're not talking Gentlemen Jack or Single Barrel. I'd be afraid to know what they cost here.

The other impediment is that if you are caught, your ass is getting smoked. The penalties can be severe—loss of rank, pay, leave, etc. Not to mention what a dirtbag you would be if you were drunk and a call came in for a 911 mission and your teammates were at risk for your inability to perform because you got liquored up. It would be SWI—shooting while intoxicated. Not good.

Personally, I love to drink. There is nothing better than some good-quality Magic Hat or Rogue ales for a card game or when heading out to the bars. I've also been known to spend the extra dollars on some Single Barrel Jack Daniel's when the mood is right. But here, it's just not an option.

So until I'm home for good, and done with this war, Jack and Bud and Jim will remain missing in action. If you see them and they ask where the soldiers have gone, let them know we will be back home soon and will be sure to look them up.

WHEN DISOBEYING AN ORDER IS JUST COMMON SENSE

During a mission south of Ghazni, our ANA and ANP allies discovered a series of IEDs and mines that had been placed along our route. Normal standard operating procedures in the U.S. Army are to secure the site, *not* handle or disrupt the IEDs, and notify EOD (Explosive Ordnance Disposal).

In contrast, the normal ANA procedure for handling IEDs is to monkey around with the stuff and do everything you can to blow yourself up. Handling IEDs, moving them, and even disassembling them for parts (to later be sold at the bazaar) are common.

So it was no surprise that an ANA soldier approached our Humvee with a burlap sack containing heavy, bulky items. Fearing the worst, I told him to stop, gently place the sack on the ground, and walk away from it. Instead, he carelessly dumped out the contents at my feet. Before me was a treasure trove of armed antitank mines, claymores, and the wire and battery packs to detonate them remotely.

I immediately got on the radio and reported the find to

The mines, IED materials, and RPG launcher that were dumped at my feet.

the War Eagle TOC. The officer on the other end meant well—with over twenty years of enlisted and officer service, he is experienced and offers a wealth of knowledge in all matters military. But he is also known for making problematic tactical decisions in the field. Whenever danger lurked, he would suddenly get "stuck on stupid" and issue orders that bordered on suicidal.

When apprised of the situation regarding our pile of armed IEDs, his original plan was sound. Call EOD and wait in place until they arrive to take the IEDs. But when the EOD unit failed to show up at our position, he then ordered the IEDs to be delivered by us to the nearest EOD unit, which was along our route home to our FOB. No problem. Then he ordered us to place the sack inside the Humvee and transport the items to EOD. My alarm bells went off, and

Corporal Polanski's eyes opened in horror as he heard this order over the radio.

Knowing that the ride back to the EOD unit was a bone-jarring, bouncing one rivaling that of any roller coaster, I politely questioned his order. "Sir, do you think it's a good idea to put these armed devices *inside* the Humvee, given that they will be tossed around like juggling balls?"

"Yeah, the Humvee is armored, so you will be okay," was his response. More shock on Ski's face.

"But, sir, the explosives will be *inside* the armor, not outside of it," I replied. "If the IEDs explode, all the blast will be contained *inside* the armor, turning us to Swiss cheese."

"Just put them in there, you will be fine. Put a backpack or a sandbag on it to add more protection." Ski's shock was quickly turning to outrage. I was more dumbfounded by the complete lack of logic than by the fact I could be pulverized in the not too distant future.

Ski and I looked at each other, and we were both thinking the same thing: Is he serious? He must be kidding. A backpack or a sandbag would have no effect in preventing the IEDs from blowing us to pieces. I pushed the issue further, but at this point, the man we called Deathwish on the other end of the radio was getting angry and made it clear what his wishes were. I suggested to him some safer alternatives for moving the IEDs, but he rejected them out of hand. The conversation was over; he had given me my orders and expected me to comply.

Ski and Vandy (Specialist Ryan Van De Walker), the third ETT teammate on board the Humvee for this mission, were basically ready to mutiny. They refused to drive in the Humvee with these assorted active IEDs bouncing around in the seat next to us. But they had nothing to worry about, because I wasn't going to let that happen.

The Army teaches us all the slogan "Everyone is a safety officer," and it's everyone's obligation to stop an unsafe act, regardless of how high-ranking the person perpetrating the act.

In the end, some wheeling and dealing was done with the ANA commander on the scene with us. He understood our predicament, grabbed the sack of IEDs, and tossed them into the back of his pickup truck. The IEDs made it safely to the EOD unit, where they were later destroyed, and no one was the worse for my disobeying a direct order.

CULTURE SHOCK

INSHALLAH

Anyone who comes to Afghanistan is immediately introduced to the concept of "Inshallah." Roughly translated it means "If God wills it." In a nutshell, it's how Afghans, as well as other Muslims, use religion to deal with the hardships, violence, and chaos of life around them. In America, we also have religious influences in our daily lives, but none of them compare to the degree that Inshallah shapes an Afghan's daily life.

Recently an Afghan soldier walked by a U.S.-owned pickup truck and saw some valuable property locked inside it: a DVD player. Then he saw a rock lying next to the vehicle, and "Inshallah!" God must have put that rock there and the DVD player there, and it was God's will for him to smash the window and snatch the DVD player. While this seems far-fetched, it was the Afghan soldier's alibi when he was caught in possession of the stolen loot. He confidently, and without shame, explained that he was only acting out God's plan to get him a DVD player.

Now, in America, any cop hearing this story would laugh

and probably smack the thief in the head a couple times. But here it's a plausible justification that can shield one from negative consequences. To go against Inshallah can be seen as going against the will of God. We would call out this excuse as shameful, but here it's a crutch that allows corruption and dishonesty, and retards Afghan society in too many ways to count.

We as ETTs see this daily when performing our military duties with the ANA. Afghan soldiers, for the most part, view training exercises as folly and a momentous waste of time. In their minds, God rules the battlefield, not the soldiers and bullets. God determines if you survive combat, not training. Whether or not your bullets hit the target has nothing to do with practice on the rifle range, it's purely God directing the bullets. As a result, getting the ANA to the rifle range is harder than herding cats.

While it's hard to maintain objectivity when I see Inshallah being used to shield bad behavior, the honest truth is that many Americans are buying into it as well. We use it to rationalize keeping the extra equipment or supplies that accidentally get delivered to us, and that we stash away in a connex for future use, all the while denying we ever saw it. We use it to explain the blind luck and utter randomness of the drama that unfolds around us. When your vehicle goes unscathed on a long and dangerous patrol route, and your buddy's gets blasted by an IED the next day, in the back of your head you say, "Inshallah—it wasn't my time, someone somewhere was looking out for me!" And out here, where the threat is so high, and the consequences of being in the wrong place at the wrong time are so dire, having a little Inshallah on your side can't hurt.

DIAL A DATE

My interpreter Hameed was sitting in my hooch, waiting for me to finish writing a document that he would need to translate into Dari. As I made my last edits, his phone rang, and I saw his face light up when he looked at the incoming number.

He began to have an upbeat and animated conversation. I could hear the voice of a young woman on the other end of the phone, and I assumed it to be his sister.

Intrigued, I studied his face as he spoke. He was smiling from ear to ear, and blushing like a schoolboy about to get his first kiss. The unrelenting stress of being an interpreter in a combat zone had vanished.

After about ten minutes he concluded his call, and I immediately asked him who he'd been conversing with.

He told me a bittersweet story of romance. The young woman he had been talking to had called him one evening the week before. She was a complete stranger, and had been dialing phone numbers randomly, hoping a young man would answer. When she reached Hameed on his cell phone, he was a more than willing participant in her dial-a-date game.

Even though she didn't even tell him her name in their initial conversations, Hameed excitedly embraced this blind opportunity for long-distance love. Given the extreme restrictions on male and female interaction in Afghanistan, it should be no surprise that within minutes of this anonymous conversation, these two young adults had declared themselves boyfriend and girlfriend.

With no chance of ever meeting each other, they had convincingly fallen in love. We all know love when we see it, regardless of our cultural lenses, and I could see that Hameed was knee-deep in it. He was literally skipping with joy as we walked over to visit an Afghan Army officer, and he exclaimed with pleasure that he had spent over $20 on phone calls to her in the last week alone, a sign of the seriousness of his commitment.

I asked him what they talked about, and he said they talked about their day, and their plans for tomorrow. There was little to nothing touching on love and romance, yet this bland fare of conversation, in an Afghan context, was pure titillation.

What did the future hold for Hameed and his girlfriend? At best, their telephonic romance could blossom into an exchange of email addresses, and if they were really adventurous, a cell phone camera photo could be sent. But these seemingly innocent acts would put the woman at great risk. In Afghanistan, such a communication would be seen as a violation of family honor, with real and severe consequences. I'm reminded of an Afghan woman who met a secret admirer on a public park bench in broad daylight, shared a few moments of polite conversation, and left without ever having made any physical contact. When her family discovered this had happened, she was murdered by her brothers for dishonor.

Over the next few weeks Hameed continued to receive

Hameed the combat interpreter and the ANA passing out winter clothing, toys, and candy donations that I had collected from friends and supporters back home in the U.S.A.

calls from his girlfriend. But the frequency of these calls decreased, and Hameed became resigned to the fact that his cell phone tryst had run its course. With no chance of developing further, their small flame of love was eventually extinguished. Hameed returned to the gray and draining life of daily combat patrols and tedious translations of Army documents, and his girlfriend either lost her phone privileges or moved on to a new anonymous phone number.

But while it lasted, Hameed was a man in love, a million miles away from the war and poverty that define daily life in Afghanistan. It remains true, even on a cell phone, in a war-ravaged land, with an anonymous partner, that it is better to have loved and lost than never to have loved at all.

A SUMMER ROAD TRIP

You know you're dehydrated when your piss is orange. Or you're so dizzy that you're swerving off the road, scaring the hell out of your gunner. Or when your passengers repeatedly ask you "Are you okay?" because the vehicle is proceeding erratically down Ring Road. I could go on and on.

The up-armored Humvee weighs in at about twelve thousand pounds—six tons of lethal, armored mobility. Pushing this monster up the road is a powerful engine that generates lots of heat. And in our IED-rich environment, windows are *never* opened to let the airflow in unless you want your brains to end up on the windshield. I've seen brains blasted onto windshields, and it's not a pretty sight.

Reaching 110 degrees Fahrenheit is normal in the summer here. I've already written about the layers of clothing and protective gear that we are smothered in even in these temperatures. Luckily, Uncle Sam had a plan to negate the interior vehicle heat problem—superpowered air-conditioning. This AC can make the heat manageable, but only if it works, which wasn't the case for us today on our four-hour drive from Kabul to Ghazni.

Due to a maintenance problem, we could not use the AC without running the risk of blowing the radiator. The net result was that it got hot in our Humvee.

Actually, "got hot" does not do justice to the kind of heat we were suffering through. Let's quantify it. One of the guys had a crystal LED wristwatch with a thermostat in it. When the watch hit 152 degrees Fahrenheit, it just crapped out. So it's possible it got even warmer than that.

The heat from the engine is passed throughout the vehicle by convection and conduction, so in addition to the ovenlike air, all the metal parts of the vehicle heat up. Door handles, radios, brackets, console, all get so hot it literally will burn your hands if you make prolonged contact. You find yourself in contorted, uncomfortable positions while seated just to avoid touching any metal parts. Luckily, the steering wheel is plastic!

Our last and only line of defense is to aggressively hydrate. On a long, hot drive, it's normal for a full Humvee crew to go through three cases of bottled water. That's about thirteen bottles per man. You may be thinking, "Ahhh, cool water, nothing beats the heat like cool water." Correct, except the water we have in the Humvee is also being exposed to the 150-degree temperatures. It's like drinking hot tea, minus the tea. Drinking water at these temperatures is a chore, not a reward.

Prior to beginning our movement back to Ghazni, I placed some bottles on the radio mount for easy access during the drive. The plastic got warped from the heat, and the water tasted like burnt plastic. Mmm . . . refreshing!

By the time we arrived at our FOB, I felt like I was on fire. I stumbled out of the Humvee and threw off my helmet and body armor. I felt like I had escaped from a sauna gone haywire. My cloth seat had a sweat body print soaked into it, like a post-nuke Nagasaki silhouette burned onto a wall.

But like everything else here, soldiers can put a positive spin on any hardship to keep it from wearing us down. There is a silver lining to this hot-box predicament: Winter is only months away, and at least I know I'll be toasty warm in my Humvee when the snow starts to fly.

WE HAVE ALL THE WATCHES, THEY HAVE ALL THE TIME

If history has taught us anything about making war in Afghanistan, it is that the invading force always under-estimates the resolve, intelligence, and abilities of the seemingly dysfunctional and backward Afghan people.

And when things start to go poorly for the invader, as they did for the armies of Alexander, the British Empire, the Soviet Union, and even our current NATO Coalition, the lack of military progress is seen as a result of having an in-adequate number of forces. Like our antecedents, we will pile in more troops.

Sending an additional thirty thousand soldiers may seem like a rational approach to fighting and defeating the growing Taliban insurgency, but it misses a simple truth. As the Afghans like to say: "You Americans may have all the watches, but we Afghans have all the time."

This simple Afghan proverb reveals the basic flaw in our current approach to victory. We have spent the lion's share of our efforts on military force, relying on our high-tech weapons and gadgetry to win influence over the people, all the while fumbling with minimally funded reconstruction efforts. Statistics show that on average, the per capita money spent on Afghan reconstruction was about $57, while the per capita amount spent in Bosnia was $580; in Iraq, it was an even higher $1,000 per capita.

It's not that it was wrong to use force to overthrow the Taliban; it's that once we did this, we basically considered the war won and rested on our laurels. I think some people also assumed the Afghan people were too ignorant, too corrupt, or frankly too unimportant to merit the type of investment that is needed in order to develop the country.

I personally witnessed many examples of how we underestimated the Afghan people. During my time in Paktika with the Blackfoot ETT team, one of my tasks was mentoring the Afghan battalion's administrative staff section. Upon my arrival, I found out that the United States government had purchased the battalion brand-new computers to help modernize their daily work. So I was puzzled as to why the computers remained locked away, collecting dust, while the Afghan soldiers worked with no typewriters, no copiers, and only a motley collection of stubby pencils and wrinkled pads of paper.

When I asked my American commanders why the computers hadn't been issued to the Afghans, I was told that they weren't going to get them because they didn't know how to use them, and "would just break them, sell them, or steal them." These American commanders, like many others in country, didn't see the value of teaching the Afghans computer skills. Ultimately, they saw such efforts as futile and as a distraction from the main military goal of killing the enemy and winning the war.

In fairness to their position, they could cite many examples of equipment being stolen or poorly managed by the

ANA. But had any of my commanders bothered to visit the administrative section I was mentoring, they would have found that in the dingy, dark office, among its disheveled and grimy-looking staff, were some highly intelligent, computer-proficient soldiers who were motivated to improve their battalion but lacked any tools or resources with which to do so.

With some arm-twisting, I was able to get a computer out of storage and into the hands of this section, and within weeks they had left the Stone Age of handwriting everything to become a modern office capable of printing, copying, and distributing reports in a timely fashion. Their record keeping improved, their efficiency improved, and ultimately, the productivity of the battalion improved.

Despite this small-scale success story, I believe we are still reluctant to accept that the Afghans are capable of modernizing, and we are resorting to more military force to solve the country's perceived problems. This plays right into the enemy's hands.

Ultimately, the positive contributions of our Western cultural values, and the modernizing capabilities of our technologies, are lost in the dust storm of violence. Our watches mark the passage of eight years of war in Afghanistan. And despite sincere efforts to help the Afghans, we scratch our heads as the very people we thought we saved are today turning back to the Taliban.

It is these efforts to modernize, investing in human capital and physical infrastructure, which will cause the Taliban to wither away. I can't count the number of times villagers would express their need for roads, wells, seeds, and animal medical services to us. The appeal for security from the Taliban was usually far down on their list of requests.

In the end, given a choice between the West and the

Taliban, the vast majority of Afghans will want the Internet, exposure to Western culture, cell phones, music, arts and culture, and the more moderate and liberal approach to governance of the current Afghan Government. They already embrace these things in the privacy of their homes, but are less likely to do so in public because we have alienated many of them with our heavy-handed resort to violence as the main weapon for defeating the Taliban. Continuing to emphasize a military solution to Afghanistan's current problems will only doom another generation of foreign soldiers to failure.

INFORMATIONAL DETRITUS
FROM THE WAR ZONE

I n the last week, nothing has happened here. I shouldn't complain, but the boredom of winter is slowly turning into cabin fever. The workload has been light lately due to the weather and some big-picture shuffling and policy changes going on at echelons well above our pay grade.

So I thought I would take this moment to share with you some tidbits of information that alone don't really merit any mention, but together in a quick list format might help you figure out what it's like here. Just a few small pieces of the Afghan puzzle. Some of these are administrative, some are comical, some are grisly. But they are all part of the Afghan experience.

1. They built a new chow hall on the FOB here in Paktika. Once a week, we get served lobster tails, steaks, and crab legs for dinner. Top-notch stuff. It's a complete change from the food situation we had back in Ghazni. There it was ramen noodles and Afghan flat bread with an occasion freeze-dried hamburger patty.

2. Once a month, one of us ETTs gets a big plastic bag of money from the Army: $25,000, to be exact. It's given to us in Afghanis, the Afghan currency. This month it's my turn to get the money bag. I'm authorized to spend it to improve the living conditions here on the FOB for us ETTs and Afghan soldiers, and to employ local nationals, which in turn benefits the local economy. The program has a funny name: "FOO." It stands for Field Ordering Officer. Every month a couple million dollars of Uncle Sam's money is disbursed this way to every ETT team in the country. For the most part, it is spent wisely and benefits the war effort, but a lot of it is lost in waste, fraud, and abuse.

3. Some ingenious soldiers have figured out how to feed their iPods into the high-tech headphone communication systems we have in our Humvees. Music sounds *a lot* better when you're driving down mined roads, and it helps to take your mind off the risks.

4. Many people ask me about Internet access here on the Afghan Army bases. We have rinky-dink satellite Internet, and when it snows or rains, it goes dead. It's also painfully slow. It can take three minutes just to open up a picture in an email.

5. I am responsible for managing ten Afghan interpreters here in Paktika. It's like a second job, being their boss and tracking pay, attendance, etc. I don't get any fringe benefits for having an extra ten employees who gripe and complain and weasel about their daily affairs.

They also bring me the daily rumor of new American laws passed by Congress for combat interpreters to get permission to go to the United States. The rumor mill never stops churning out these stories of easy visas to America, where the streets are paved with gold.

6. The AK-47, carried by our Afghan National Army soldiers, literally hollows out the skulls of Taliban when they score a head shot. I don't know where the brain goes, but it's usually nowhere to be found. Just a big empty cave masquerading as a skull. It's a surreal sight to see. A man lies there staring at you with eyes wide open, but the side of his head is gone and there is nothing inside except a cracked skull.

7. All Afghan cell phones are "pay as you go"—i.e., you buy scratch-off tickets, call in the code on the back, and get your allotted amount of minutes. While there are two major Afghan wireless companies here now (with a third on the way), I've yet to see anything resembling a "cell phone plan" like we have in the States.

A WORLD WITHOUT WOMEN

Think of all the people you met today, or talked to, or had interactions with. Now remove half of them—erase half of what you learned, saw, shared, and experienced from your mind. This half just ceased to exist. The result is that your day is now only half as educational, enjoyable, and worthwhile.

Here in rural Afghanistan I travel every street, at all times of day and night, in small villages and in the country, but I'm only meeting half the people I should be meeting. The half I'm missing is invisible. The half that's missing is the women.

There are none in taxis, on buses, on bicycles, motorcycles, or cars. There are none working in stores, in the military, farming, building roads or houses. There are none walking on the streets.

On occasion, you catch a glimpse of the "blue ghosts"— my personal term for Afghan women hidden in their burkhas. These soft blue shrouds billow in the wind and give a ghostlike appearance to the female human forms they con-

Women are seen in public only in large urban centers, and even then they are usually concealed under blue burkhas.

ceal. The blue ghosts are ethereal reminders of the fairer sex. Technically, there is a woman underneath, but practically there is nothing feminine to prove it. All we see is a blue wisp of cloth, with no face, voice, or name. The women are gone, and Afghan men don't seem to notice that their country is only half as present, enjoyable, and productive as it should be.

AFGHAN PORN

Today, I wandered into what the ETTs call ANA Land, the portion of the base where the ANA soldiers live. While we as ETTs live on an ANA FOB, we have our own small area that we call home. In a sense it's a mild form of segregation. We've got ETT Land, and they've got ANA Land.

I had some business to conduct with my ANA counterparts, and made my way toward the wooden huts that they use both as administrative offices and personal living quarters. I knocked on the door, was called in, and sat down for some precursory small talk and snacks. The grimy and dark hut had a small wood-burning stove for heat, multiple bunk beds for sleeping, large wall lockers, and a television with a DVD player for entertainment. It's standard fare for any ANA living quarters.

As I conducted business with my Afghan counterpart, other Afghan soldiers came and went, drinking cups of *chai* and conducting official and personal business. All of which was normal and to be expected.

But when a soldier came in holding a DVD up in the air, the mood perked up, and I could tell something was afoot. He slipped it into the DVD player and all small talk ceased. I looked at my interpreter, whose smile betrayed the guilty pleasure about to be enjoyed.

Guys are guys, and the language barrier was broken by their expressions of anticipation. I've seen it a hundred times among U.S. soldiers—someone had some porn and was about to share.

The screen came alive with a woman dancing evocatively and seductively. Except upon closer review, it became clear that this woman was in fact a man. He was surrounded by a crowd of at least fifty Afghan men of all ages and ethnicities, all gazing at him with starry eyes. They sat in orderly rows around the dancer, smoking cigarettes and waving handfuls of money, much like American men seated at a strip club would do.

Compared with your standard MTV video, the dance and the costume were mild and tame. Nothing was revealing, nothing shocking, nothing explicitly sexual. The only exposed skin was the hands, face, and feet of the dancer.

But in an Afghan context, this video was triple-X. Since it's forbidden for women to dance like this, let alone in public uncovered at all, videos like this one fill the gap for "sexual" entertainment.

Apparently here in Afghanistan, there is a tradition of the *bachabas*, best translated as the "boy toucher." Young men, obviously homosexual, assume the public persona of women, dress like them, talk like them, and act like them. They make a living through public shows like that on the DVD as well as by prostitution, though not all are prostitutes.

While homosexuality is strictly forbidden in Afghanistan, there appears to be a cultural caveat that allows the *bachabas* to remain somewhat public and accepted in society without repercussion.

The society has banished women from the public eye. Men are literally condemned to a female-free existence until they marry. And even then, sexual activity is pretty conservative. Afghans who I have talked to have unanimously condemned premarital sex, oral sex, and masturbation as "sins," and deny practicing these vices themselves. Yet many of these same men have discreetly asked many an ETT if they can borrow porn DVDs and magazines.

I am reminded of a comical moment when I first came to Afghanistan in 2004 as a civilian on a humanitarian mission. I was at an Internet café in Kabul, and in walked a Muslim clergyman. He received a lot of attention from the café workers, who obviously knew he was an important local mullah. He sat next to me in the neighboring stall, and began typing away like everyone else in the room. When I was getting up to leave, I must confess I was curious to see what a mullah would be surfing on the Internet, and had to hold back an audible gasp when I saw that in the privacy of his computer stall, his monitor was filled with pictures of hard-core sex acts.

Which brings us back to the *bachabas*. As a result of the high level of sexual repression in Afghanistan, the natural human need for sex and sexual stimulation is in a pressure cooker with no release valve.

Through some cultural loophole, these cross-dressing *bachabas* are permitted, and their services purchased, by a society that condemns pretty much any access to women. Perhaps it's a tacit recognition of the indestructible human need for sex. A woman cannot appear in public, but a cross-dressing gay prostitute is permitted.

A double standard appears to be present, but my aim is not to criticize. We in America have our fair share of sexual double standards. We have a government that blocked development and access to the morning-after pill, yet allows erectile dysfunction medicines to permeate our print and television media. We have right-wing preachers campaigning for antigay ballot amendments who then get caught smoking crystal meth with gay prostitutes.

I think the moral of the story, both for Americans and Afghans, is that all efforts to stifle and repress sexual activity just pushes human desire into other outlets. It only further dehumanizes us, makes us take up costumes and personae that may not really meet our natural needs, but serve as second-rate substitutes.

All business ground to a halt in the ANA hut when the

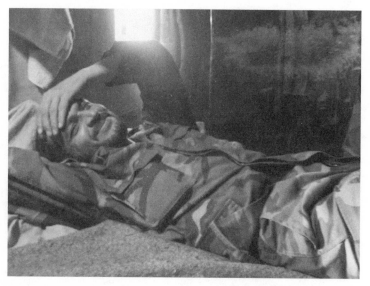

Caught in the act: An ANA soldier watching "Afghan porn" in his barracks.

bachabas DVD went on. So I said farewell, and as I left I had to chuckle to myself. The soldiers were transfixed by this mild, if not boring, Afghan display of "porn." It's only a matter of time before some Jenna Jameson DVDs find their way into ANA hands, and once they do, I have a feeling the *bachabas* DVDs will be collecting a lot of dust.

WOMEN OF KYRGYZSTAN

I've recently discovered a dirty little secret that further rubs salt in the wounds of us downrange ETTs who live on grubby, ramshackle postage-stamp-sized bases. This secret was revealed to me during a transient stop in Bagram, the largest of the metropolis bases, the crown jewel of comfort and amenities for Coalition soldiers in Afghanistan. Bagram is the realm of pleasure, with manicures, twenty-four-hour movies, and a Dairy Queen. While Rome burns, one can quench one's thirst with fresh fruit smoothies within the safe confines of Bagram Air Force Base.

But the secret I'm going to disclose really isn't a secret at all. It's something open and public. But it remains relatively unknown among the dirty, unwashed masses of ETTs who live downrange. The secret, and all its pleasures, can be bought for $7.25 U.S.

Inside a subdued, sandy-brown one-story metal structure, located on the remote northern section of the base, dwell the women of Kyrgyzstan. There are no hints that reveal the treats that await within this nondescript structure, except for a small red, white, and blue square sign, posted outside the white entrance door. The sign says AAFES BARBER SHOP. *AAFES*—pronounced "a-fees"—is the Army Air Force Exchange Service, an administrative body that runs all the shops on Army bases, such as clothing sales, the commissary, etc.

Needing a haircut, I decided to stop in for a quick buzz. Ninety minutes later, I walked out tingling with an excitement I hadn't felt in a long time here in Afghanistan.

The first sign that this place wasn't the "normal" AAFES barbershop was the loud techno-emo music that greeted me as I entered. A large TV set playing Russian MTV videos of slinky, scantily clad blondes was positioned for all waiting customers to view. The second thing that told me I wasn't in Kansas anymore was the stable of young, attractive, and equally evocatively clad women working the barbershop floor. They all chattered away in some foreign language (probably Russian) while they walked back and forth like runway models.

Exotic would be an appropriate description of their ethnic background—some looked like classic Russian women, but most were an attractive mix of Asian and European ancestry. They all had one thing in common: tight low-ride jeans and belly shirts, revealing more nubile flesh than I had seen in six months of downrange duty.

I sat down, awaiting my turn for a haircut. An awkward silence prevailed among the soldiers seated there. We all looked like the cat that ate the canary. As each new person arrived and took a seat, we'd exchange a quick glance, and share a discreet grin. Among young female-deprived and sex-starved soldiers, no words were necessary. The expression on our faces said it all.

Time passed, and I noticed on the near wall a large red

flag with a yellow emblem. I'd seen this flag before, but where? Then I remembered, it was the national flag of Kyrgyzstan. The people there were pretty much Russian-speaking and of mixed Asian and Russian ancestry. The riddle of the women's origins was solved.

About this time I also became aware of the fact that these women were not giving the normal military haircuts. In most AAFES barbershops, you are usually done and gone after ten minutes. But here, soldiers were spending at least forty minutes waiting for a haircut, and another forty in the barber's chair. It turns out that the $7.25 price tag got you a lot more than just a quick trim.

The haircut was slow, careful, and well above the care and attention level normally given to the average military trim. Then, over a professional hair salon marble sink, came

Women from Kyrgyzstan walk along the main street of Bagram Air Base.

a nice, slow shampoo and head massage, with warm water and slender feminine fingers. And if that wasn't enough, when this was done, back into the barber chair you went for an extended head, neck, and shoulder massage.

Nirvana.

Now, for those of you who expected some sordid tale of sexual activity and indiscretion in an old metal building tucked in the corner of the base, I'm sorry to let you down. This is where the story ends. Nothing of the sort goes down with the girls of Kyrgyzstan. No Army regulations were violated, and no relationships were breached. But for me, for any of us here who are deprived of any interaction with women for months, these simple pleasures have a morale-boosting effect on our female-starved brains that is as good as sex, and well worth $7.25.

ARAB VACATION DAY

I've left Afghanistan on a four-day R & R pass. Part of the benefits package of spending a year getting shot at is that the Army gives us this short holiday in a peaceful and beautiful part of the Arab world. Here in the rich oil kingdom of Qatar, one finds himself quickly surrounded by shiny SUVs, shopping malls, girls in bikinis by the pool, and the opportunity to legally drink the nectar of the gods: BEER!

For months, I've been quietly celebrating the fact that I would be traveling to Qatar as part of my authorized four-day pass. I fantasized about how good a cold beer would taste, and how sweet the views would be at poolside. The bikini-clad Air Force girls would be a nice substitution for the dusty head-to-toe blue burkhas of Afghan women. I couldn't wait.

Yet on my first day here, I didn't visit the pool, and I didn't drink any beer. I didn't go shopping, and I didn't look at any women. The whole scene, the whole feel of it all, as much as I had craved it for months, was too foreign for me

Captain Tupper sightseeing in Qatar. In the background, a row of hunting birds sit tethered on posts.

to actually go enjoy it. I felt alienated and unwelcome, like I didn't belong there, and I somehow convinced myself it would be wrong to enjoy it. Instead, I fell victim to exhaustion, both real and perceived, and I slept straight through the sun and evening socializing hours.

I've got three days left to enjoy the sun and peace of Qatar. This is my spring training for going home, and so far, I'm batting .000.

Day two of my pass was a better day. I finally mustered the courage to belly up to the bar, and getting a couple beers in my system seemed to be just the oil that this engine needed. It broke some rust off the old "Fun Meter," and cranked up the life enjoyment factor.

So yes, to quote the great Ernest Hemingway, "the sun also rises." Unfortunately, in Qatar, when it rises the temps shoot up to about 120 degrees. But that's why they make air-conditioning. And the best place to enjoy air-conditioning is on a nice stroll through a shopping mall. Without weapons, without body armor, hell, without anything military on my person at all except my crew cut and my Combat Infantryman Badge tattoo.

The trip to the mall was nice, for many reasons. It capped off a day of sightseeing, camel markets, ocean vistas, and delicious Arabic food.

While wandering in the giant shopping mall, I encountered a few things worth mentioning. First was the huge skating rink in the center of the mall. Yes, an ice-skating rink! Qatar has more money than they know what to do with, so when the idea came up for a huge skating rink in the middle of the 120-degree desert, I'm sure the planners shrugged their shoulders and said, "Why not?"

Another view that is strange to Western eyes is the women in exquisite silk black burkhas. These are not the dusty and weathered women of Afghanistan in blue burkhas. These are the pampered and wealthy Arab wives, mistresses, and daughters of millionaires. Beneath these black silk burkhas are gold and diamond jewelry, exquisite makeup and expensive perfumes, and Prada and Gucci outfits. If you watch carefully, as they shop for Oakley sunglasses or sample the newest shades of makeup, the veil comes down to reveal goddesses who lack for no cosmetic product or spa service.

But most revealing and enlightening about my four-day pass in Qatar was my accidental conversation with an Egyptian man. He ran a small store selling Egyptian items and knickknacks. He was my age (mid-thirties), and had a pudgy face and an American-style baseball cap on. He and I struck up an accidental political discussion while I admired a great little Anubis statuette. I always had an affinity for Anubis. He was such a badass!

Anyway, this Egyptian man was a working-class "Mohammed," just another Joe on the street who was lucky enough to get a visa to work in Qatar and escape the poverty of modern-day Egypt.

He didn't hide his strong Muslim faith, nor his pride in his Egyptian homeland. But he also didn't hide a streak of common sense and good judgment that was refreshing to hear from someone so different from me. As we talked, we inevitably broached the subjects of the war in Iraq, and of the Palestinian-Israeli conflict. His positions were simple and clear:

The Jews were good businessmen and good neighbors when they lived among the Egyptians. He blamed the British for fomenting Arab-Jewish hostilities in the 1940s, and he wished that the Jews never left Egypt, as they were strong contributors to the economy and the progress of the country. This was not what I expected to hear from a young Muslim man.

As it pertained to Iraq, he said the obvious. The war was a mistake, and a tragic blunder. He said the Iraqi people deserved the civil war they now had, because their country was like a field infested with worms and moths. The only way to cure it of this blight was to burn the field to the ground. He said America should leave, and let the Iraqis burn down these fields and replant something in healthy soil.

As for Afghanistan, he laughed. He said some people are just too crazy, and he said al-Qaeda was beyond discussion, as there was nothing logical or Muslim about them.

He said he understood why Americans seemed to hate Muslims, and feared Islam. One day, he watched an Internet video of one of the executions by some fringe group in Iraq, where they beheaded a prisoner. He said if he was American, he too would fear Muslims. But he impressed on me that this was totally contrary to the teachings of Islam, and he was embarrassed by it. I told him it was a two-way street—Americans couldn't be so lazy as to see that video and write off all Muslims as killers. It was our responsibility to balance this violent image with tolerant people such as him.

It was a wonderful twenty minutes spent sharing opinions with a complete stranger. He and I shared no common experiences or places or friends, yet we both agreed, on a simple level, on what was good and bad about the world. I decided on buying the Anubis statuette, because I hoped it would always remind me of this tolerant Egyptian man.

DOGS OF WAR

FOB Ghazni is built upon the ruins of an old Russian Air Force base. More accurately, it is a cob-job recycling of the ruins that the Russians left behind. The effect is some sort of postapocalyptic Afghan warrior tribe existing among the ruins of a war gone by. Think *Escape from New York* or *The Road Warrior*. While there has been some modest construction on the FOB recently, many of the buildings left decaying by the Russians are now currently occupied by the ANA as barracks and office space.

Scattered across the landscape are reminders of the previous war's legacy: corroded barbed wire, rusting Russian artillery and antiaircraft pieces, crumbling concrete guard huts, countless brass artillery shell casings, and unfortunately, unexploded ordnance. So when we walk through the large airstrip area, extreme caution must be practiced to avoid old mines and bombs. While this may seem dangerous, it's only our secondary safety concern on the FOB. The first and foremost danger is the dogs.

Breeding in the abandoned fighting positions lining the FOB's expansive perimeter are packs of wild, untamed, and

FOB Ghazni: An old Russian guard post now houses one of the wild dogs that patrol the vast expanse of the FOB's old Russian airstrip.

hostile dogs. Big dogs, small dogs, white dogs, black dogs, dogs with mange, and dogs that look so cute, you would want to ship them home as family pets back in America (which, believe it or not, some soldiers here, like my ETT buddy Vandy, have done).

For the most part, the dogs are fearful and flee when you approach. But they don't go far because they have lived their whole lives inside this barbed-wire and earthen-walled FOB. It's their home as much as ours. But if the mood is right, and the pack is motivated enough, they will mount an impressive attack on any soldiers daring enough to traverse "their" area. How the dogs define "their" territory is unknown and impossible to predict. You only know you have crossed the line when they attack.

It's our policy to always carry one weapon at all times, so it should go without saying that quite a few dogs have been shot down while making a defiant Pickett's Charge on an ETT or ANA soldier. Lately, others have been culled in a methodical program of canine cleansing, and the packs have been reduced from about eighty dogs to twenty. When I tell people back home about this dog shooting, they act repulsed and upset. "You guys shot dogs?!" Yet, when I tell them we shot Taliban, they seem to celebrate the death of humans. That's one for the theologians and psychologists to ponder.

Complete eradication of the dogs is not our goal or desire. The dogs do serve a purpose, as an additional security barrier from any would-be attackers. It's much easier to sneak past sleepy Afghan soldiers than it is to infiltrate past a pack of dogs. Their barking is a foolproof alarm system that makes sneaking over the barbed wire and into our FOB impossible. They may not realize it, and it may not seem like it when the dogs are chasing you away, but an enemy of your enemy is your friend.

WELCOME TO PAKTIKA

I've recently arrived at my new FOB in Paktika Province. The FOB, which is formally known as FOB Rushmore, is located about forty miles to the southeast of Ghazni. The good news is that I've been reunited with many of my original Twenty-seventh Brigade Combat Team ETT buddies. We trained up together in Camp Shelby but were split up once we arrived in country. The bad news is that I've left Ski, Vandy, Komar, and Cain. So it's a mixed bag, but it's part of a big-picture plan to reunite ETT teams that were split up initially.

Although I'm bummed to leave my buddies in Ghazni, there are quite a few fringe benefits of being on FOB Rushmore. First, we have HBO! We have a satellite TV dish here that is run through India, so while there are many American channels, all the commercials are for Indian products. Apparently, there is Pizza Hut in India, and they have some whacky pizza toppings like curry, kebobs, etc. It sounds crazy but looks really good.

Today was my first full day here, and it was a productive

Captain Tupper poses next to the "Welcome to Paktika" sign.

one. We had a "snitch" (informer) come to our FOB and provide us with information on a cache of enemy matériel. So after about an hour of driving, we arrived at the alleged cache spot. Then, as snitches often do, he revealed that he didn't know exactly where the cache was, but he knew a guy in town who did. So back to town to grab this other guy, who upon arrival said he didn't know where it was either, but his dad knew. So back again to town to get the dad, who, as you can guess, didn't know where it was either. But through some effective persuasion and threats of detention, eventually the son revealed the location of the cache—and out came the shovels. About three feet into the sandy earth, the shovels started hitting metal objects, and four hours later, an impressive mound of hundreds of cases of ammunition had been excavated.

So a long day ended with some measurable progress. Every bullet we take from the Taliban is one less they can shoot at us.

THE SUN NEVER SHINES ON PAKTIKA

One good thing about being transferred to my new Paktika FOB is the Navy cooks who make us three meals a day. The walk from the Mobile Kitchen Trailer (a small covered cooking area on wheels) to my hooch, where we eat, is short—only about sixty meters. But this distance is long enough that the hot meals get drenched in the dirty raindrops that seem to constantly fall over our base. By the time I reach my living area, the food is cooled and covered by the grimy rain. The precipitation, which started clean and pure in the white clouds above, gets turned gray by the pollutants from trucks belching smoke and oil, and the piles of burning trash and feces that dot the Afghan landscape.

I've been here in Paktika for about a week now, and the difference from Ghazni is palpable. Ghazni Province, the land of eternal sun and endless blue skies, is in stark contrast to my new stomping grounds. Gray clouds, cold rains, and muddy gloom seem to be the fabric of Paktika Province. This contrast is also revealed in the disposition of the Afghan people here.

I spent six months in Ghazni and saw nothing but smiling faces greeting our convoys as we moved about, searching for the elusive but ever-present Taliban and al-Qaeda fighters. Even in areas run and controlled by the Taliban, people, especially children, would wave, give the thumbs-up, and approach us for small talk.

Here, literally on my first Paktika drive to my new base, I had an Afghan man give me "the finger," something unheard of in Ghazni. Ghazni appears to be in the midst of an economic boom: new shops are opening up daily, and the buzz of commercial activity is the backdrop to a city growing by leaps and bounds. Here in Paktika, it appears that progress is in reverse. Shops, roads, and homes all appear to be in a slow state of decay and desperation. I haven't been here long enough to gauge the reasons for this, but it's visible even to a newcomer like me.

Yesterday, during a mission back toward Ghazni Province, I found myself shrouded by clouds and a soft rain, looking for an elusive Taliban leader with my new ETT and ANA team. People hid in their mud homes, and no one came out to greet us or investigate what was going on. While we waited for our ANA to finish searching some compounds during this fruitless wild-goose chase, I had time to gaze to the north, where I could see Ghazni City and its outlying districts. Sure enough, they were all bathing in warm sunlight and blue skies.

POEM

I found myself one evening laid out on the trunk of my Humvee. The sun had long since set, and in the dusk I could see both American and ANA soldiers unwinding from a long and active day of missions during Operation Mountain Fury, one of the largest operations to ever be conducted in the 203rd Eastern Corps.

As I lay on the trunk, I was overwhelmed by the beauty of the sights, sounds, and smells that surrounded our little bivouac. I grabbed a small blue chemical light stick, my dog-eared notebook, and began to write. This is the first and only poem I wrote in my yearlong tour.

"An Afghan Night of One Thousand Senses"

The day was hot.
Offensive.
Inhospitable.
Now the night arrives.

Cooling breezes.
Scents of a dry earth . . .
Mixed with pungent hashish . . . warm flatbread . . .
    mutton and beans.
All woven and mixed together with each of my
    inhalations.
The air's gentle waves pass through my uniform,
    soaked in sweat.
Now it feels dry, new, fresh
Washed clean by the wind.
The sky to the west dances with heat lightning.
Overhead, it is a sea of distant white stars.
To the east, this tranquility is broken by artillery guns
Firing their illumination shells into the expanse of
    blackness.
The shells rise from the guns—invisible.
Then, without warning, explode into orbs of yellow
    light.
Below, the sleeping ground is awoken and lit by these
    man-made falling stars.
Soon, they fade, and the night reclaims its
    dominance.
Hidden in a valley painted black by the night, and
    untouched by these yellow orbs
A well pump's engine beats a constant rhythmic
    "thump thump thump"
A mechanical lullaby for the night.
Escorting children into sleep, like a mother's
    heartbeat
In a womb of sandy fields.
One by one, my senses are tranquilized by this
    Afghan night.
The ethereal caress of the wind.

The firm grip of the earth.
The distant rhythm of war and industry.
The smells of nourishment and pleasure.
The night's act is complete.
My eyes close.
Satiation.

A WARM-BLOODED AND
SOLAR-POWERED ENEMY

It was easy to miss. No one noticed it as the Blackfoot ETTs of 4/2/203 Combat Support Kandak loaded up the crew-served weapons and ammunition onto our vehicles on a crisp but still warm November morning. We packed up the already crowded interior of our up-armored Humvees with medic bags, commo equipment, and "pogie bait" (food) for our long drive to central Afghanistan.

It was Sergeant C who saw it first. "Holy shit! Look at those mountains."

Mountains? My first thought was that they'd been there for countless millennia, and would probably be there for many millennia more. Unchanged. What could have happened overnight to garner the surprised attention of Sergeant C? "They're fucking covered in snow! Check it out!"

We all gazed to the east, and sure enough, the backdrop to our last six months of work had been painted white. Now, to the casual reader, such an occurrence may seem mundane, hardly worthy of comment. Snow comes and goes. It's part of the natural cycle of the seasons. It happens in America, it happens here. So what?

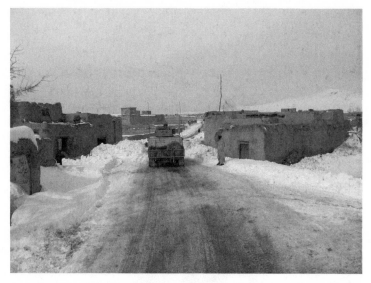

The first major snowfall of the winter in Sharana, Paktika.

But to us, this sight had almost religious implications.

The snow, and what it brought—cold, bitter winds, slippery surfaces, and frozen extremities—was like an army of white that had arrived to route the enemy from these hilly hiding places.

The snow would be able to do something that forty thousand Coalition soldiers were unable to do. It would drive the enemy out of his unlimited hillside redoubts, and deny him sanctuary from which to launch his attacks throughout eastern Afghanistan.

The Taliban are solar-powered fighters. We all are, to different extents. The hot summer air allows for men at war to sustain themselves in these high-elevation hiding places. Remote, difficult to access, and easy to defend, mountains are a friend to any guerrilla army anywhere across the globe. And these mountains were no different—an endless source of well-concealed caves that provide living quarters for hundreds of Taliban and al-Qaeda fighters.

But Old Man Winter changes all this. With a swift white wave of his hand, these mountains become a place where men who remain will die from exposure in a brutally short time. The enemy, although hardy and strong, do not get issued cold-weather gear. They don't get Gore-Tex–lined outer garments, nor silk undergarments designed to retain heat and release moisture. No winter boots, no gloves, no fleece caps and jackets. And most important, no helicopters to deliver firewood, food, and water. And absent these luxuries, they must leave their mountain camps and descend to lower ground. And in the lowlands, we can find them, fix them, and finish them.

Throughout the summer, the cat-and-mouse game was as predictable as it was violent. The Taliban came out of their mountain hideouts to conduct operations. We would get intel on where they were and go hunting. It would end in one of two ways: We would either engage them and inflict horrible losses on their soldiers, or they would be able to get back to their mountains and disappear. They would only reappear at a time and place of their choosing to sow IEDs, ambushes, and terror.

Those distant white caps that Sergeant C had spotted changed everything. The rules of the game were radically altered overnight. The solar-powered warriors of the Taliban now have three choices:

1. Die in the mountains from exposure.
2. Die in the lowlands from our forces.
3. Flee to a safe harbor—i.e., Pakistan.

All the choices are in our favor. And being somewhat rational men, the majority of the Taliban are choosing the third option. An estimate I heard from a well-placed source at the Second Brigade's ETT intel section was that 75 percent of the enemy will leave here and winter over in Pakistan. While this still leaves a substantial force capable of killing throughout the winter, it means a drastic reduction in the amount of violence the enemy can muster during the coming months.

Once in Pakistan, they can hibernate in an area that has little to no government influence or authority: the Federated Tribal Areas of Pakistan. In this part of the country, there is no government, no war on terror, no desire to hunt down and eradicate terrorist elements. This part of Pakistan should be called Pashtun-istan because Pashtunwali rules. Pashtunwali is a cultural tradition of loyalty to, and sanctuary for, any visitor or persecuted person. Pashtunwali trumps any and all mandates or laws established by a governmental body.

So this is where the Taliban are going—in groups as small as one man or as large as a dozen. Leaving their weapons in caves or buried underground, or hidden in the mud homes of supporters, they make this anonymous journey east into Pakistan, appearing as simple laborers or travelers. Upon arrival, they will be given sanctuary, food, and they will receive further training in the war against the government of Afghanistan and the Coalition Forces who are here to help secure this government.

But on our level, just a bunch of Blackfoot ETTs getting ready to go out on a mission, we just stare at the snowcapped peaks and embrace all the implications. Welcome to Afghanistan, Old Man Winter, you're not a day too soon. . . .

MY HOLIDAY APPEAL

Greetings to all—I hope this holiday season is keeping you in good spirits. Whatever your religion of choice is, I wish you good times, and maybe even some quality adult beverages to make those office parties and family gatherings more "manageable."

On a more sobering note, I wanted to tell you about something I recently witnessed here while on patrol through a small village that left me teary-eyed and depressed—something that profoundly affected me.

It's wintertime here, cold, damp, and harsh. I go out on these missions in four to six layers of clothing, including high-tech Gore-Tex and Thinsulate, yet I inevitably end up a shivering mass of flesh and body armor.

Despite the cold, I commonly see children, by the dozens, wearing the same attire they wore in the summertime—a thin cotton shirt and pants. No hats, gloves, and in many cases, *barefoot*! Trekking through snow and ice, these children go about their daily business apparently oblivious to the cold. But we all know they are not oblivious to it; they are suffering through it.

As a result of my holiday appeal blog, my living quarters in Sharana were soon overflowing with hundreds of boxes of donations sent from the U.S.A.

Many people back home have expressed a desire to send me care packages for the holidays. Honestly, I have everything I need here already. So I'd ask those of you who wish to send me something to instead send me a package of items for these kids.

It's really easy. There is no need to spend money on this (beyond postage). If you go through your closets, grab up some old socks, gloves, mittens, hats, T-shirts, ANYTHING, and throw them in a box and mail them to me. Within three miles of our base, there are literally hundreds of children who have no cold-weather clothing.

Other items that go over well are old teddy bears, stuffed animals, Beanie Babies, etc. Afghan children live a toy-free existence, and the smiles on the faces of the little boys and girls we give these out to are priceless.

Now, I'll add a comment to this appeal: every hat, teddy bear, or pair of socks we hand out is a tactical defeat for the Taliban. The bad guys go through these same villages and preach how the Americans are evil and here to ruin Afghan lives, culture, and religion. Yet when we show up and pass out these gifts, it literally destroys this image of the "Ugly American." Every child and family that receives these donated items is less inclined to believe the Taliban's propaganda. Every gift we hand out makes our job here *safer*. These gifts are more effective at winning the people's support than any bullets we shoot at the enemy. And you, thousands of miles from Afghanistan, can be an effective, constructive, and nonlethal combatant in our fight against the Taliban.

Thanks, and Happy Holidays.

Follow-up to the Holiday Appeal:

I have been overwhelmed since I posted my "Holiday Appeal" blog, first with emails from people wanting to send me packages, and now the packages themselves, which have started arriving here in the dozens. Literally hundreds of you have emailed asking for my address to send me items for the kids here, and many of these emails promised packages from multiple sources. So all I can say is THANKS! Today was our first patrol where I was able to start handing out items en masse to the kids in the village we visited. Boxes from Connecticut, Massachusetts, and Colorado were distributed today to about seventy-five kids.

WINTER PARALYSIS

If you've ever griped because a snowplow was late clearing your street after a hefty snowstorm, imagine the scene here in Paktika Province. Eighteen inches of snow have totally obscured the roads—there are no signs or posts to designate the difference between a road and the ditches that run alongside it. Everything is an unbroken field of white.

With the best of intentions, our ETT group went out into this frozen wilderness and inadvertently shut down the country's only paved highway. We created the traffic jam of all traffic jams, adding to the snowy dysfunction caused by this large winter storm.

We were on a mission to Kabul, and had to travel along Ring Road, the only paved highway connecting all the major cities of Afghanistan. The snowstorm had slowed traffic substantially, and when we arrived at a tricky portion high up in a mountain pass, there were about forty vehicles from either direction slipping and sliding past one another. In our haste to clear this logjam, we ended up sticking one of our Humvees deep in a snow-filled ditch.

A winter view along Ring Road, Wardak Province, on the drive to Kabul.

Our attempts to recover the vehicle proved futile, and we had to enlist a large civilian truck to pull it out. All the while, the traffic was totally stopped by this recovery attempt, and the crowds of vehicles and people to our north and south continued to grow rapidly. By the time we had pulled the Humvee out of the ditch, there were hundreds of Afghans out milling about, watching the Americans at work. Within half an hour, these masses had formed into impromptu tea parties. Others took to more solitary activities to pass the time—prayer, naps, or talking on cell phones.

Despite the lack of outward signs of hostility, security always remains our number-one priority. With our limited personnel, we put into effect a cordon around our vehicles, and tried to keep the curious onlookers out of our area.

But our attempts at crowd control fizzled, as we were unable to maintain any semblance of a security perimeter.

Despite our menacing looks and surplus of weapons, Afghans found the melodrama too irresistible to watch from the front row, and the crowds kept pushing in closer and closer to the action. At one point, a young U.S. soldier from our Sec For (Security Forces), who had spent an hour sliding around, trying to keep people back, momentarily showed his frustration and let himself fall, arms fully extended, into a snowbank. There he made a snow angel. The crowd erupted in laughter. Sometimes humor is the best weapon. Some people began backing up, more out of sympathy for his hopeless attempt at doing his job than out of fear of his gun.

Fortunately for our ETT convoy, there were no suicide bombers among the crowd, and the Afghans themselves were taking it all in stride. In America, horns would have been honking, people would have been swearing, fistfights would have broken out. But here, among the sunny, snowy panorama, our crowd of interrupted travelers played the role of curious onlookers—the whole event, how it originated, how it would be solved, was all just *inshallah*. God clearly had willed this mishap as part of His master plan. Given Allah's clear creation of this logjam, there was no point in getting angry about it. The delay was serving some heavenly purpose, even if this purpose remained unknown to all who were present.

In the end, our vehicle was removed from its snowy trap with the help of the Afghans, and we mounted up and continued on to Kabul. Hundreds of Afghan cars, buses, and trucks slowly began to move, free now to continue their own slow march through the snow.

MIDNIGHT WINTER VISITORS

The first night, they came before midnight. A distant rumble, a "whop whop whop" that you feel in your diaphragm before you hear it in your head. The unmistakable reverberation of air being violently ripped and thrust down to maintain the flight of an ugly, insectlike black steel and aluminum creature.

"Apache!"

My hooch mate woke me up with his shout from behind the thin plywood board that separates his "room" from my "room." His thick Southern drawl accentuated the raw thrill of the approach of this death machine.

The Apache AH-64 attack helicopter is the king of battle in Afghanistan. It can—and does—chase down fleeing enemy over hilltops, in speeding vehicles, even hiding in caves and mud compounds. With its high-tech night vision and infra-red capabilities, it hunts better in the night than in the day-time. And in the darkness, it's invisible in the sky, just a vague noise that seems to be here and there simultaneously. It only reveals its true position when one sees the explosions of the rockets or chain guns releasing a quick and violent death onto its target.

And on this night it was hunting in our neighborhood. Immediately all our heart rates picked up as we chased away any last remnants of sleep from our cloudy heads. Apaches don't joyride at this hour, in this part of the country, without a reason. So we all sat up in our beds, silent, listening for telltale signs of escalation—flaring engines, rocket explosions, the burping sound of the chain gun.

But the Apache just kept circling, fading away (perhaps leaving?), only to turn and fly back over our FOB. This back-and-forth flight lasted about thirty minutes. Then the chopper was gone.

Its departure without a climax left us all in an unresolved and unfulfilled state. Like a lover teased but not satisfied.

The next night, the visit came a little after midnight. I was deep in a pharmaceutically induced sleep when I heard a noise that cut through the drugged slumber like a knife.

A fast ripping sound, like the sky being torn open, jerked me out of bed. It was not the slow, methodical thump of the Apache. This midnight visitor was either something really good or really bad.

The 107mm rocket is the enemy's weapon of choice for indirect attacks on FOBs all across Afghanistan. It makes a buzzing noise as it flies through the sky. Our FOB has been rocketed numerous times since the summer, so hearing this noise jerked me up out of bed. I waited for impact.

With a cringe on my face, I braced for the explosion. But there was no *boom*. This was a good sign.

Then I heard the same sound again, and knew it was not rockets. It was CAS, or close air support, ripping the skies high above our FOB. It was most likely U.S. F-16s, but possibly French Mirages. Either way, CAS was on station above us, burning holes in the clouds, passing in big wagon-wheel circles high up in the moonlit winter sky. Occasionally they would swoop down lower and lower, as if feeling out the ground below, looking for some elusive target.

They stayed on station for ninety minutes and left.

I stayed awake until sunrise.

The following night, again, we had another aerial visitor. Our friend the Apache, perhaps as unfulfilled as we had been by his previous night visit, had returned. Maybe it was back because it was eager to share its lethal caress. Who knows? We sure don't.

JITTERS

L ately, the weather here has been a refreshing break from the monthlong deep freeze. The mercury has crawled up into the forties, turning hard-packed ice into an endless sea of brown, oatmeal mud. This warmth has also begun to defrost the war. Both sides seem affected by it. We are all starting to feel a tingling in our cold extremities as we sense a slow but steady increase in the heat of war.

Our senses are going through a spring training of sorts. Evenings, which during the winter have been dominated by deep intellectual discussions of women and alcohol, are now focused on whether we will get attacked tonight. Our "situational awareness" is returning to game-day form. Guns are getting cleaned more frequently. Some are sleeping in their uniforms, ready for the expected attack that will come in the night.

The enemy is also flexing his muscles. Reports of attempted (and thwarted) infiltrations back into Afghanistan from Pakistan are more frequent. And today, just up the road from us, a classic IED-initiated ambush followed by direct arms fire was sprung on an ETT-ANA convoy by the Taliban. Just like in summer, the radio was alive with reports of this gunfight.

Another factor that has gotten us back on edge is the recent extension of a Tenth Mountain Brigade here in country. As we enter the last quarter of our deployment, we're all cautiously optimistic we won't get extended. But the fact remains that over three thousand soldiers who had done their time here were told to stay for an encore three months.

Our anxiety over a tour extension is best understood through the story of these Tenth Mountain soldiers, stuck here for at least another ninety days. Some of the soldiers in this brigade literally made it all the way back to Fort Drum, New York, and were hours into their welcome-home ceremony, when they were told to immediately get back on the plane and return to Afghanistan.

When, in this happy scene of families reunited, the announcement was made to get back on the plane, the Army wives literally rioted, and Military Police had to be called in to quell the disturbance. Food was thrown, chairs scattered, and tables were overturned in the unrest.

FAREWELL, FALLEN COMRADES

DEATH OF A WAR EAGLE

This one hurts a lot. In mid-September, about halfway through my yearlong tour, our War Eagle ETT team suffered its first U.S. KIA. Sergeant First Class Deghand had spent five months as a member of the team in Ghazni, and had just been transferred to a different ANA infantry battalion due to interpersonal squabbles among the team's leadership. Deg, as he was better known on our War Eagle team, was a straight shooter and didn't put up with their bullshit. He would tell our commander and his head NCO when they were wrong and wouldn't mince words. As a result, he was shipped off to a different ETT team by our leadership. On the day he left Ghazni for his new base, we all went around giving him hugs and trash-talking our team leaders for letting this happen. Deg wore a pair of black Oakley sunglasses that did a poor job of concealing his tears as they rolled down his face. He wasn't the only guy crying that day.

Sergeant First Class Bernard Deghand was a good old boy from Kansas whose drawl at times was harder to understand than an Afghan speaking Pashto. He was killed in action on September 15 by small-arms fire. He was a teammate, and for a short stint, when Corporal Polanski was away on leave, he was my partner.

Deg was a great guy. He couldn't spell worth a lick at times, but could put a hurting on me on the chessboard with ease. He understood this war, and how to win it, both on the battlefield and in his everyday interactions with Afghans.

He was the first guy out on missions to get invited for *chai* by village elders, and he never left a village with any money in his pockets. His standard operating procedure was to go to the nearest shop and buy as many toys, pens, and snacks as he could to give to the army of kids who would instinctively follow him. He was the Pied Piper of goodwill and friendship, and all the children and adults picked up on this immediately. He just had that easygoing knack, even in Taliban-infested villages, which was something very few of us could pull off naturally.

On the battlefield, he was lethal. I can't tell you how many times I saw him lead the charge against enemy positions. At times, he would shame the timid Afghan soldiers into action. He would maneuver by himself on an enemy position, exposing himself to the brunt of enemy gunfire, pausing only to stop and look back at the ANA soldiers. His expression transcended all language barriers. His eyes would say, *This is your country! This is your fight! Get the hell up here with me and let's get these bastards!* And without fail, within moments, Deg would have a squad of ANA soldiers by his side.

And then—watch out—the bad guys were gonna be falling like raindrops.

"Deg" was old enough to be a father figure to us, but

Sergeant First Class Bernard Deghand, a.k.a. Deg, was posthumously promoted to master sergeant after he was killed in Spera, Afghanistan.

young enough to be our brother. He embodied both the wisdom of age and the innocence of youth. He was cranky and boisterous, yet soft-spoken when he knew he was wrong, or needed advice. He never disowned a mistake; he owned up without hesitation.

I spoke to him the night before his death via cell phone, and we exchanged our normal barrage of infantry greetings (curse-laden insults and jabs). He mentioned he was leaving for a long mission in the morning, but he wanted to ensure there were no loose ends on some projects we were still working on together.

The last thing I said to him was, "Be safe."

FADING AWAY

The physical disappearance of people here takes many forms. In part and in whole, mentally, physically, spiritually, people disappear. We become thinner, shallower, hollowed out by the grind of the war.

Some of us disappear in our totality—because we are killed or injured so seriously that we just disappear on a helicopter, never to be seen again. We leave behind an empty bunk and piles of disheveled equipment and personal items. A mass of dirty gear and memories serves as a poor substitute for the person snatched from us.

Twice I have had to inventory footlockers full of gear and weapons choked with carbon and cordite residue, and throw out bloody uniforms and equipment. I clean everything up, package them nicely, and ship them back home to the States. It's an eerie process that is best done with a partner. Done alone, the silence of the missing soldier's quarters is deafening.

Some of us disappear in pieces: injuries that remove nonessential parts and chunks of our physical forms. Others

disappear physically in slower, more drawn-out ways. Perhaps I best exemplify the latter category. I watch my physical form get slimmer, as weight evaporates off me like
sweat. I was always tall and relatively thin, yet in the first
four months here I lost thirty pounds. My heavy equipment
grows even more burdensome as I lose body and muscle
mass. No matter what I do, I've been unable to stem this
weight loss. It could be nerves, it could be the daily 110-
degree heat, it could be some illness, I don't know. But I'm
plagued by a nagging, irrational feeling that I'll continue to
shed my form until one morning, I'm gone. Just gone.

Captain Tupper at Bagram Air Base.

EXHALE

It's just past midnight. The wheels of the C-17 that will take me on the first leg of a long journey home for leave began rumbling down the tarmac at Bagram Air Force Base. The bouncing and bone-rattling vibrations of the aircraft remind me of the hundreds of miles of rough and mined roads I've traveled since my arrival here in Afghanistan. Shades of nervousness and anxiety creep into what should be a celebratory moment.

The noise of the aircraft straining to gain flight drowns out all attempts at conversation. Even now, when I should be enjoying this temporary reprieve from the war, I find myself reflecting back on past moments when the whir and pulse of combat drowned out any hope of communication.

I'm reminded of the fact that some of us leave here without ever feeling what I'm feeling at this moment of pre-flight. These mixed emotions of relief and anxiety. I think of Sergeant First Class Deghand, who never had a moment like this. He was killed weeks before his much-deserved R & R leave.

And then, as my thoughts drift to him, his example of bravery and friendship, the aircraft is silenced as the wheels finally leave the rough ground below. I'm on the verge of breaking down. I wipe tears from my eyes, and yet at this precise emotional moment, I become aware of a sea of smiling young faces, fellow soldiers who recognize that they have just left the rough and violent grasp of Afghanistan. Airborne, we climb into a peaceful sea of stars and silence. Finally, after long months of holding my breath, I exhale.

A SHRUG AND A SMILE

Being here in Afghanistan, as a soldier who regularly goes into harm's way, who has had his life extended by flukes, near misses, and improbable odds, who has lost close friends and seen others maimed in combat, I have been altered to the core.

I accept it as normal to be changed like this. I'm running with it, not away from it.

But I have to confess something, which on the surface may seem irrational and problematic.

I love it here. I don't say this to sound cocky or full of bravado. I know it's a love that is self-destroying and is unsustainable, like a heroin addiction.

But the drama, the thrill, the risk, the camaraderie, the simple enjoyment of everything mundane, celebrating it as a gift to the survivors, it's difficult to downplay.

When I was home on leave, a day didn't go by without me hearing the following comment: "I don't know how you guys do it. I would go crazy. I wouldn't be able to handle killing and people trying to kill me." In response, all I could do was shrug and smile.

Shrug and smile.

It's all I could muster on the spot. I had no real immedi-ate response. There is no easy response.

When I was home on leave, people described me as de-pressed, anxious, distant, erratic, irritable, removed. All of which was probably accurate. While home, I felt like I was watching a black-and-white movie of myself. Nothing seemed real. It seemed like whatever I did, no matter how risky or ill-advised, the consequences wouldn't really affect me. After all, it was just a movie.

And this movie, which lasted until I stepped off the plane on my return to Afghanistan, seemed pretty boring to me. In hindsight, the truth was the opposite; I engaged in more unsafe, dangerous, and irresponsible acts during those weeks at home on leave than I had done in the previous thirty-five years of civilian life.

But once I stepped off the plane, and I breathed in the smoky, dusty air, and saw Apache helicopters taking off on some dangerous and *in extremis* mission, it was like I was plugged back into life. The movie ended. Credits rolled. The screen went black and I was released to a full-color version of life. I was back in the driver's seat. I didn't know where I was going, but I was at least behind the wheel.

This war has both disconnected me from my life and provided me with a new one. New goals, desires, and hopes. A legitimate, palpable reincarnation of myself. Hopefully for the better. The naysayers and skeptics would argue this is unlikely, but I have an almost religious faith in an optimis-tic outcome.

But I cannot downplay the damage that has been caused to me, and that I have unfairly passed on to others. These changes have closed some doors, but opened new ones. The war, and more important the impact on me, has caused stress among my family, ended my marriage, and shuffled my life in ways that will radically alter my day-to-day existence when I return home.

But it's also created opportunities for me to pursue new options in life, in work, in love, in just the mundane day-to-day priorities and activities. And despite the damage done to my mind and body here, I'm confident these changes allow me the opportunity to become a better person, a better father, a better friend. Like I said, I'm changed, and I'm running with it.

All these reflections are perhaps what I should have said to those who couldn't imagine what it's like here. It's a response as complex as it is personal. It's draining to reflect on this. It's draining to write it out in words.

A shrug and a smile was a lot easier to deliver.

SEPTEMBER 11 COMA

Yesterday was the big five-year anniversary of September 11, but honestly, I didn't feel a thing. I guess I should. I'm from New York. I had friends directly impacted by the New York City attack. As I recall that warm, sunny summer morning, I was awakened by my wife, who told me that the buildings had been hit by airplanes, and within an hour I was told to report to my armory, as the 1/108 New York National Guard infantry battalion had been mobilized to respond to the attacks.

Later, I would spend almost a month at Ground Zero, guarding the workers as they slowly removed debris and rebuilt the underground infrastructure. But honestly, on September 11, 2006, here in Afghanistan I felt no connectivity to that place or those events.

What I see now has little to no relationship to bin Laden and al-Qaeda. Sure, their soldiers and bomb makers are here, but this war is now about Afghan issues, and September 11, 2001, is but a footnote in the bloody chapters being written in these follow-on years.

If I was home, I think I would have felt differently about this anniversary. But being here, I see a population experiencing their own daily 9/11s every day for the last thirty years. Our loss back home seems like a drop in the bucket compared to the violence and death that the Afghans have experienced over decades. This Afghan loss, misery, and suffering amounts to a structure of sorrow that dwarves the Twin Towers.

For the last month, I've been able to sleep about three hours a night at best. But last night, on this eve of the anniversary of our national American tragedy, I slept a dreamless sleep of twelve hours.

R.I.P. SSG PHANEUF

The following is the official DOD notice for SSG Phaneuf:

"The Department of Defense announced today the death of a soldier who was supporting Operation Enduring Freedom.

"Staff Sgt. Joseph E. Phaneuf, 38, of Eastford, Conn., died Dec. 15 in Mehtar Lam, Afghanistan, of injuries suffered when an improvised explosive device detonated near his HMMWV during combat operations. He was assigned to the 1st Battalion, 102nd Infantry Brigade, Hartford, Conn."

Staff Sgt. Phaneuf was a veteran of the "Summer of Hell" we all went through in Ghazni. He lived over at the Provincial Reconstruction Team, just down the road from our ANA FOB. He was a regular out on the PRT's quick response force that was sent out to rescue our War Eagle ETTs all summer. He was a confident, impressive NCO, and had the swagger and good looks that made you feel safer whenever he was around.

I received word of his death a few days ago from CPT

Komar. Komar was even more shaken up by Phaneuf's death because he had sat next to him while traveling home for leave. He said the Taliban had made some super-IED that involved five fifty-five-gallon drums filled with explosives, buried deep underground, and equally spaced so as to blow up five Humvees, all in one strike. Fortunately, only one of the drums exploded, sparing the other Humvees in Phaneuf's patrol. But the one that did blow up hit Phaneuf's vehicle dead-on. Komar said it was so powerful that there was barely anything left of Phaneuf when the dust settled.

PIECES IN THE SNOW

The streets, the fields, the market bazaar, everything as far as the eye could see was covered in a coat of pure white. During the night a snowstorm had passed through our corner of Paktika, dropping just enough snow to cover all the mud and dirt and garbage that paints the landscape of the town.

I stood on the main road of this normally bustling bazaar, in this expanse of pure white, staring at a mysteriously vibrant pink and red object. Around me, there were no footprints disturbing the fresh powder except my own. It appeared as if this strange object had been dropped from the sky onto this patch of snow. It lay there in simple repose—thin, fibrous strands splayed like a peacock's tail feathers along its top. At the base, a stiff stalk of white segments adorned with bright red dollops.

After the initial distraction of marveling at its intricate

makeup, I refocused on my original purpose in approaching it. I needed to identify what it was. Having done so, I turned and walked back to my Humvee.

It was the neck stem of a human spine, blasted 150 meters in the air from the site of a suicide bombing.

Thirty minutes earlier, I was in the middle of a slow, frustrating meeting with my commander and our ANA counterparts, arguing over attendance numbers. A very subtle vibration passed through our meeting room. It was gentle and unassuming. With no one even mentioning the distant thud, we all continued our conversation, until one of my ETT teammates ran into the room and yelled, "We're rolling! There's been an explosion in the bazaar!"

Minutes later, I stood as part of a chaotic scene, ANA soldiers and ETTs trying to organize a wide cordon around the blast site, with rumors spreading of a VBIED ("vehicle-borne improvised explosive device"—a car bomb) still in play, and confusion in sorting out the dead, the wounded, and the lucky.

These initial moments were tense. Scattered in the intersection were seven unoccupied vehicles. Any one could be a secondary explosive device intended to kill the first responders, a classic enemy tactic. As we tried to get a grasp on what had happened and what needed to be done, we all were within the lethal blast radius of even a small car bomb.

I found myself nervous, but ironically fighting back a smile. I kept expecting a fiery white light to instantly wash me away.

Bang . . .

Torn car metal.

Flame.

But when none of this transpired, I was happy as a kid

Sharana ground zero: Moments after the suicide bomber detonated himself, all that remains is the blackened road and pieces of his body scattered in all directions.

on Christmas morning. And every second that there was no explosion, my grin continued to grow.

This reaction seemed even more out of place, given the random burned and twisted body parts scattered about as I walked through the scene. But no one noticed me. Each of us was in our own little world, trying to process the remaining risks and the results of this suicide blast.

The events were fairly easy to reconstruct. A lone suicide bomber had walked up to a group of ANA soldiers who had congregated at a street intersection outside of our base. He detonated his explosive vest, which instantly scattered his mortal remains in a truly random pattern. Ground zero was a large blackened circle where he had stood. The blast instantly evaporated the snow and burned the ground below it. His head flew straight up, landing about twenty meters away on the hood of a white Toyota station wagon. It rolled off onto the ground, leaving a red smudge and streak across the hood.

His heart landed about fifty meters in the opposite direction. It sat there, in perfect condition, as if carefully removed from the chest by a surgeon's delicate cuts. An ANA soldier walked by and kicked it down the road like a small soccer ball, a gesture of disgust at this suicide attack.

In my sector of the cordon, I stumbled across the aforementioned spine segment, and wandering another twenty meters, I found the rest of the spine, the remaining ribs cracked and splayed like old, mummified fingernails.

That's where I spent my day. Standing beside my Humvee, watching the sun cross the sky and eventually set. A cold, silent street remained, devoid of people, activity, and life. Shadows slowly crawled across the blast site like ghosts looking for something they had left behind.

Aside from the cold soldiers who remained to secure the scene for the bomb experts, the only witnesses to our grim daylong vigil were gaunt dogs, who, smelling the fresh meat on the wind, came to steal a meal from the bones of the bomber.

The silence of this morbid scene was broken at sunset by gunshots, and the horrible yelps of a dog caught sniffing around the bomber's head. Shot but not yet dead, the dog was howling as if it cursed the irony of locating food, only to be struck down for its lucky find.

Up until this moment, I had spent my day staring at parts of the human body that are normally hidden from view. I had poked at a large sheet of flesh, covered in goose bumps from lying flat in the cold snow. I had spent twenty minutes within the kill radius of a car that was reported to be loaded with explosives. None of this fazed me in the slightest.

But this dog's continued cries, echoing off the cold and silent marketplace, hit me like an emotional bomb. They were as painful and solemn as any noise I've ever heard. It's what bothered me the most about the day.

SKI GOES HOME

Ski's time here is over. He's on his way home to New Jersey. Our survival through countless near-miss bullets, RPGs, rockets, mines, and IEDs is even more difficult to comprehend without him next to me. His smile after the fact always seemed to disarm the danger we faced together. Now that he is gone, I feel a little more vulnerable knowing he's not here to watch my back.

Corporal Polanski left Afghanistan with a chest full of medals, from the Purple Heart to the Bronze Star to the Combat Infantryman Badge. But Ski would be the first to tell you they aren't why he did anything here.

Ski, the skinny, laid-back kid from Jersey, did everything because it was the right thing to do. His priority was always to keep me, and the Afghan soldiers we served with, out of danger, even when this meant putting himself in danger.

Before Ski left Ghazni, a formation was held with the Third Infantry Company. Ski gave a quick farewell to the Afghan men we had grown to love in our time with them. Many a tear could be seen on the cheeks of these weathered

Ghazni Province: Our last mission together in Afghanistan.

combat veterans. To me, these tears are symbolic of the cruel irony of war. Hidden among the destruction and death we inflict on our fellow man, there are moments and people and actions that show the incredible potential of humanity. Every day people are transformed into heroes, giving all they have over and over for the welfare of their brothers.

While this war has scarred Ski and me in ways only combat veterans will ever understand, I feel like I came out ahead on this experience. The chance to share this fellowship with Ski has made the sacrifices and scars worthwhile.

ALIVE IN YOUR MIND'S EYE

This is a story about two men. Both are brave, committed soldiers. Each has a long and distinguished military record. Both are likable, selfless, and humorous. They are the kind of guys you'd want as a neighbor, a drinking buddy, a teammate on a sports team, or a brother. Both are stubborn in their onset of middle age. It would be dishonest to say they are perfect. We all have our character flaws, and these two are no exception. But the balance sheet on their personal and moral fiber weighs heavily in their favor.

They are good men pretty much every day, all day.

One is American, and the other is Afghan.

And unfortunately, at the end of this story, one man lives, and the other man dies.

Ali Raza makes his own introduction. At first glance, he appears like a large bear walking on hind legs. Gruff, barrel-chested, a hulking man ruggedly assembled from head to toe. His face is like a map of old battlefields, with a network of scars weaving through his black beard. Ali Raza is a veteran of nine years of intense fighting during the Soviet-Afghan war, and now four more years against the Taliban. Some of his war stories from the 1980s may be a little far-fetched, but one cannot deny the scars on his body and the hardness of his warrior eyes.

The first time I met Ali Raza, he literally pulled me off the ground with the strength of his handshake. Startled by this power, I composed myself and said the first thing that came to mind: "This man is a bear!" Once this was translated into Pashto by my interpreter, Ali Raza let out a laugh that shook the mountains.

While I may have painted a picture here of a hardened veteran, I must add that Ali Raza is not a cold or cruel man. His heavy arms are equally suited for hugging his small children, and for giving them a sense of security and protection in this violent environment. And so this bear of a man goes about his military duties with all the energy and force he needs to accomplish them. Sometimes this force may be a bit overboard, but Ali Raza is honest enough to admit he is not perfect. Although he is a devout Muslim, he still fancies vodka and beer, an acquired taste developed during years fighting with the Russians. Before you judge him for this religious infraction, Ali Raza will happily show you a doctor's prescription recommending alcohol for "medicinal purposes."

In the realm of tactics, there is no ambiguity with Ali Raza. He unabashedly prefers the Russian approach to clearing enemy villages: "Bomb everyone with airplanes and artillery, and then let them rebuild a new, friendly village." (How we guarantee the future friendliness of a village we just destroyed is a simple technicality to Ali Raza, a technicality I'm still waiting to hear him explain.) The bottom line is, if you ever met Ali Raza, your immediate reaction would be simple: "I'm glad he is on *our* side!" One could only assume that if he hasn't been killed yet in decades of warfare, he's never going to be.

In some ways, Sergeant Major McLochlin shares many similarities with Ali Raza. Both are above average in size and demeanor. Sergeant Major McLochlin is perhaps one of the tallest ETTs ever to come in country. Both men have a long record of service, although McLochlin is a senior NCO, while Ali Raza is an officer.

Sergeant Major McLochlin comes from the Midwest, and volunteered for the yearlong ETT mission in order to do his part as a soldier. With his rank and time in service, he could have easily hidden under some rock back home and avoided a deployment into harm's way. But he didn't shirk his sense of duty, and he ended up here as a volunteer combatant, on the same FOB that Ali Raza and myself call home.

McLochlin never shirks the dangerous aspects of the ETT mission. He embraces the risks as if they were free of all possible negative consequences. He even goes so far as to tempt fate with his humor and sarcasm. Before missions, he jokingly tosses his cell phone to the Afghan interpreters and urges them to use it: "Here, call your Taliban friends. Tell them I'm coming for them."

Every day, Sergeant Major McLochlin volunteers for every mission. When he is not selected to go, he works back channels to get on one of the up-armored Humvee gun truck crews. A day with no mission for McLochlin is a day of lost chances to engage and destroy the enemy.

And like Ali Raza, he has a family and children back home. No one doubts a happy homecoming in the future for this loving and patriotic father.

Many bullets were fired that hot July day. All anonymously passed through time and space, and disappeared into oblivion. All except one, which struck its mark. It dove into the shadow of a soft armpit. A split second later, it passed completely through the body, came out the other side, and was gone.

Where it landed no one knows. But for that split second, this bullet left a wound that no medic or bandage could fix. The injury was gentle enough to let the wounded man sit back and realize he had been hit, but violent enough to impress upon him the fact he would likely die.

Had he been an average-sized man, the high-velocity round would have passed harmlessly above his shoulder and smashed into nothing but air and empty space. The harm inflicted by this bullet on someone smaller would have been purely psychological. A simple cracking noise, a reminder to keep one's head down.

For his comrades, who tried unsuccessfully to stop the bleeding, it must have seemed like furious seconds passing, and then he was gone. And for the dying man, time might have passed slowly, like sand through an hourglass.

Miles away, at the exact moment of his death, I sat listening to the morbid codes and phrase words being passed over the radio. Like you, I was only aware that a man was dead. His identity remained a mystery.

This story's end is not a surprise. One of these two men is dead. In fact, he's been dead now for months. Only today did chance events transpire to weave these two lives together into this story. And as I prepared to craft the ending to this sad tale, and to reveal the identity of the fallen man, I realized that it wasn't something I wanted to do. I realized that his death is only as real as I make it for you.

Both of these men are alive in your mind until I tell you one isn't. Can't you see Ali Raza hulking over his men on this chilly Afghan winter day, the steam rising from his mouth as he yells fiery insults to motivate his sluggish soldiers? And look at McLochlin, standing before the desk of his commander, pleading the case as to why he should be on today's combat patrol into a tough nearby village.

Don't they *both* still feel alive to you?

So as I write this, I find myself in a unique position to grant what I think is the wish of all soldiers, that upon our death in combat, *we are not forgotten.*

That we can live on in the minds of our comrades, our families, our friends, and even strangers. That we can be seen much like you envision my two comrades in this story—still active, still engaged, *still alive.* If we can live on in the memories of those we touched, then we can cheat the bullet's bite. And so I'm going to grant my fallen comrade this simple soldier's wish, and let him cheat the death that claimed him. I feel some solace in knowing that right here, right now, he is still alive in your mind's eye.

FAYEZ

I spent many cold nights in Afghanistan sitting on worn mats in cramped, smoky huts, drinking *chai* with Afghan and U.S. soldiers. The winter slowed down the war, and on quiet nights we pondered many things, including religion. I was the lone atheist in the group, outnumbered by equally convinced Christians and Muslims. No one ever was able to convert their opponent in these religious debates, but there was one thing that my Afghan and American friends all could agree on: that I, the godless one, was going to hell.

And then there was Fayez, one of our interpreters on FOB Rushmore in Sharana, Paktika. He was one of the most eloquent of all the interpreters in explaining the pillars of Islam. One night, I described my faith that men could do good deeds without guidance from God . . . and my fear that religion caused much of the strife we witnessed daily in Afghanistan. This was met by a chorus of condemnation from both Americans and Afghans. Fayez floored everyone that night, raising his timid voice above the ruckus, and bluntly stating that all should consider the possibility that I was right. This was a brave thing to do in a country where even today people face death for questioning Islam.

Fayez was a soft-spoken teenager who seemed out of place brandishing an AK-47. In our country, he would have been the kid in the high school drama club, too skinny to play sports and too nerdy to get a girlfriend. But in Afghanistan, his intelligence and proficiency in English meant he was on the front lines in war, earning a high salary to support his parents and siblings.

To me, Fayez was a ray of hope for the future of Afghanistan. He was intelligent, tolerant, and decent to others.

Fayez was killed while out on a routine combat patrol. The Humvee he was riding in had been hit by a devastating

Combat Interpreter
Fayez, killed in action
26 June 2008.

IED. All the American soldiers on board probably died instantly. Fayez survived the initial blast. But he was captured by the Taliban, tortured, and killed.

News like this, of a friend cut down in the summer of his youth, shakes your faith to the core. That's equally true for a person like me, who holds no religious faith. I find myself hoping that there *is* a heaven, and that Fayez is enjoying all the rewards promised in the Koran to the faithful.

It would be dishonest to say that in the shadow of his tragic and cruel death I'm now a believer in the afterlife. But I can say, if there is such a thing as heaven, Fayez surely belongs there.

FALLEN COMRADE CEREMONY

The camp's loudspeakers crackled to life with the following announcement: "Today at 1345 hours local time, a fallen comrade ceremony will be held on Disney Road [the main road on Bagram Air Base]. All soldiers available will be present for the ceremony."

Until now, the only announcements that I've heard in my week here at Bagram are warnings of an impending "controlled ordnance detonation." The warning is followed by a pregnant pause, then a *boom*, as old mines, shells, and bombs are destroyed by EOD soldiers. I'd grown used to this, even though most of the detonations occur, for some reason, in the middle of the night. I can't tell you how many times these explosions have scared the crap out of me, interrupting a relatively peaceful night's sleep.

But the fallen comrade ceremony was something new and unexpected. I'd never been present for one before, and I was morbidly curious and excited to take part. Every base conducts these, but they are done differently depending on numerous variables, so I was anticipating witnessing and participating.

At the designated time I walked to Disney Road, named for Specialist Jason A. Disney, who was killed in Afghanistan a few years ago. The sides of the road were slowly filling with soldiers, airmen, sailors, and Marines. The sun was brutal, and standing on the hot asphalt didn't help, but no one complained. There were awkward moments of silence, and nervous laughter as the crowd grew. We all fell in at proper intervals at the position of parade rest. A whisper passed through the assembled personnel, and I was made aware that the procession was making its way down Disney Road toward us. I peeked out and saw a white SUV with police lights flashing (but no siren) heading toward me. I stood back in formation, and wondered what would follow this vehicle. Color guard? High-ranking officers? A band? I had no clue.

Less than a minute later, the SUV slowly drove by me, and we were all ordered to attention, followed by the command to present arms (salute). The SUV was followed by a second white SUV with no flashing lights. Behind that was a desert-colored, open-backed Humvee.

As it passed, my eyes were drawn to what I saw lying in the back cargo area: a sturdy metallic coffin, draped in a bright, crisp American flag. The sun's bright rays brought out deep colors in the flag, deeper than the red, white, and blue I had been accustomed to. Then two more SUVs followed, and as quickly as they arrived, the procession had passed.

The vehicles turned right and headed for the air base tarmac, where the soldier's remains would be loaded onto a military aircraft and flown back to the United States for burial. And that was it.

I never found out who was in the coffin. I had heard chatter that it was a Special Forces soldier killed two days earlier. I guess in the end it didn't really matter who lay under that flag.

SECTION 5

HOME

THE "NEW NORMAL"

I spent the last year of my life as an American soldier embedded within the Afghan National Army. The time I spent away from home was both rewarding and damaging. Like the Afghan mountains we lived and fought in, my year there had emotional high peaks and low valleys. I experienced the loss of close friends, both American and Afghan. I inflicted my personal share of destruction on my enemies, and managed to avoid my own violent demise through chance, skill, and a lot of dumb luck.

And now I'm home, and my addiction to the adrenaline rush of combat euphoria is slowly being smothered by a wet blanket of safe, mundane civility. This feeling of suffocation has made my return to the safety and comfort of New York ironically uneasy. It's probably counterintuitive, but now that I'm home, what I miss the most is being back there, among my brothers in arms, dancing to the rhythm of combat.

This seemingly unhealthy longing for the danger and thrill of war would bother me more if I was experiencing it alone. But I've got plenty of company in this withdrawal drama, so it can make coping easier at times. It's like having a sponsor in Alcoholics Anonymous, someone you know you can reach out to in a pinch and get some support for your combat cravings. So in my search for the "new normal," I know I'm not alone, and that many of the men I fought side by side with in Afghanistan are experiencing the same difficulties in kicking their adrenaline habits.

I recently received an email from a close friend whom I had served with in Ghazni. It was hauntingly short, but carried the emotional weight of a ton of bricks. It simply said this:

"I would trade everything I have to be back over there."

This fine soldier has recently taken to alcohol binges and high-risk, late-night activities. Just last week I received an urgent phone call from him, and he related his most recent ill-advised adrenaline endeavor that ultimately ended with police involvement. Listening to him tell me the story on the phone was like listening to him talk on the military radio, calling in enemy contact. Instead of lecturing him on his irresponsible act, as a good sponsor and Adrenaline Rehab partner support should have done, I was guilty of feeding off his buzz, trying to capture some of his high through my phone, saluting his dangerous actions and begging for the story to continue.

Ski also calls me regularly and leaves me voice mails using our Afghan radio call signs instead of our real names. His messages include reports of fistfights with his VA counselor, being kicked out of his father's house, and weekend-long alcohol-induced blackouts.

Within days of my return home, the front page of my local newspaper reported on a recently returned Afghan vet who was arrested after a violent alcohol-induced spree. His impressive and unprovoked rampage involved extensive property damage. At its climactic peak, he climbed to the rooftop of a building and rained cement blocks onto parked cars below. Those around me joked at how this guy must have been crazy. Privately, I smiled as I envisioned this soldier, like King Kong on the Empire State Building, raining his rage and angst down on the confused civilians below who didn't understand what could drive someone to do such an act.

He probably felt like an animal in the cage of the "new normal" civilian life. He had outgrown that cage.

The advice given by mental health professionals who deal with veterans like us is to accept the fact that we will never find the euphoric heights of combat in a healthy manner here at home. We need to accept the pleasures, albeit mundane, that our lives here at home have to offer. As sound as this advice may be, for me it's still a hard reality to accept. Giving up the need for this rush of action is like abandoning a fallen comrade on the battlefield.

And any soldier will tell you, leaving behind a fallen comrade is something we just don't want to do.

THE HEAT IN DREAMS

It felt like just another day in Afghanistan. Our Humvee crew was going through all our pre-mission rituals, like we had done a hundred times before. Captain Hep was his normal stressed-out self, and was replying to the radio commo checks with short, biting responses. The unbearable heat in the Humvee didn't help to lower his tension. Neither did the fact that the AC wasn't working.

Up in the turret, the gunner leaned forward and jerked his arm back. The metallic thud of the .50 cal being charged rattled everyone in the vehicle. *Kah-chunk*. I was the driver for this mission, so for the moment I just had to make sure our IED jamming device was up and running. I got the green light signal, waited for Hep to stop transmitting on the radio, and then flashed him the thumbs-up. Now it was just a matter of waiting for all the other trucks to finish their pre-combat checks, and we could roll out.

My two hands were tightly gripping the steering wheel while all the catastrophic what-ifs of Humvee combat patrols ran through my head.

I got my first hint that something was out of the ordinary when I glanced over my shoulder and saw my girlfriend seated in the rear right seat. She held a strand of her long hair in her hand, and was inspecting it for split ends. She pouted and looked at me. Sweat ran down her forehead onto a cheek flushed red by the heat.

"It's hot in here. Why can't we open the windows?"

Seeing her sitting there in the Humvee took me by surprise, but actually hearing her voice was what awoke me from this disturbing dream. The thought of her being there, in Afghanistan, in harm's way, was enough to make me shudder and roll over onto my side.

In these few groggy seconds, I'm able to confidently say I'm not in a Humvee. I'm firmly planted in an Army-issued cot. The cot is firmly planted in one of the notoriously hot Bagram holding tents for soldiers in transit to and from Afghanistan. I feel a slight breeze on my exposed legs. The sides of the tent are rolled up, which allows for some ventilation.

In front of me, and to my sides, are rows of cots. Most of them are occupied by fellow soldiers. Like me, they are trying to pass the hours of boredom with sleep as they await their flights out of Afghanistan.

Some are successful, others are not.

Two cots down I see Sergeant First Class "C," a fellow Twenty-seventh Brigade New Yorker and teammate of mine. Despite the heat, he is wrapped in a poncho liner and is in a deep sleep.

Directly next to me is a stranger from some other unit. He is reading a magazine of some sort. I see a glossy photo of a scantily clad female on the cover, so it's probably *Maxim* or *FHM*, the literature of choice of young male soldiers.

Across from this stranger is Sergeant First Class

Deghand, or Deg as we like to call him. He is another one of my ETT teammates. He has one arm resting on his forehead, shielding his eyes from the sunlight seeping through the tent.

Good ol' Deg. It seems like it's been forever since I've gotten a chance to really talk to him. We were ETT partners for a short stint, before he was transferred to another FOB. I smile as I see him lying there, staring upward toward the sky. God, it's good to see him. We have a lot of catching up to do.

I begin to doze off again. Some time passes. An obnoxious creak is heard as someone rolls over in their Army cot. It's a noise every soldier knows. It's a noise only an Army cot can make.

More time passes.

"Are you gonna tell him?"

A stranger's voice, right next to my cot, and possibly directed at me. I ignore it.

"Hey, are you gonna tell him? He was your friend." The stranger puts special emphasis on the word "your."

I look over, and the stranger is sitting up in his cot, looking at me. He motions over toward Deg.

His casual demeanor is replaced by a look of seriousness. Now he's got my attention. Before he speaks, I already know what bad news he wants me to deliver.

"Aren't you going to tell Deg? Aren't you going to tell him that he's *dead*?"

My eyes dart from the stranger's face to Deg, who remains resting on his cot. His chest rises and falls with his relaxed breathing. It's the same chest that got shot last September. The bullet cut through all the important parts. Heart. Lungs. We heard he died on a helicopter en route to surgery.

Deg shifts his head over toward me. I see tiny specks of sweat on his face.

He smiles at me.

I smile back.

It feels so good to see him.

But the stranger is right. I should tell Deg. But I can't.

Deg and I remain locked in this silent reminiscence. He is still smiling at me. Perhaps he is remembering the practical jokes we played on our interpreters, or the nail-biting evening chess games, or the time we bought melons and shared them with everyone at that street intersection in Ghazni. We had some great times together.

Maybe he just wants to catch up on things. But I know if we start talking, I'm going to have to tell him why he can't

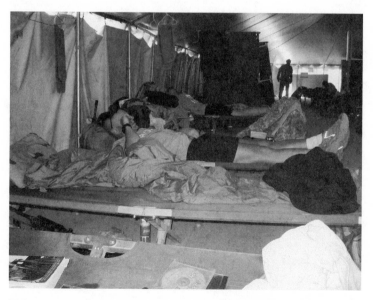

ETTs awaiting their plane ride home in the sweltering tents on Bagram Air Base.

go home. I'm going to have to give him the bad news. I close my eyes to collect my thoughts, and to muster up the courage to tell him what happened to him.

I open my eyes.

The red numbers on my alarm clock read 4:16 a.m. It's Eastern Standard Time.

NOT THE REUNION I WAS HOPING FOR

Ski and I first met on a hot summer morning in Ghazni, Afghanistan. I was inspecting one of our base's fighting positions when a tall, skinny kid with glasses and a pencil-thin mustache ambled up to me. His camouflage boonie cap sat cocked sideways on his head, and his pistol belt hung low off his hip.

He didn't salute me. He didn't even stand at parade rest. He casually reached into his pocket and pulled out his lighter and lit a cigarette. Then, with a thick Polish accent, Ski mumbled his first words to me.

"Wasssssssup, sir."

And so began our partnership as Embedded Team Trainers within the Afghan National Army. Ski was assigned as my NCO for leading and training an Afghan infantry company. In the Pashto language, and among the Afghan Army soldiers, our company was officially known as "Too-Lay-Say," which translated means Third Company. But Ski and I quickly nicknamed them "the Third Herd." This seemed appropriate, given the cloud of dust and gun smoke they kicked up whenever we rolled out on a mission. At times they acted more like a wild cattle stampede than an infantry company, but they got the job done when it mattered, so we didn't complain too much.

Our company went out on more missions, was in more combat engagements, and probably killed more enemy than any group in our battalion. Third Company was just like Ski and me: laid-back and easygoing, but serious when it was time to do the heavy lifting in combat.

We seemed to have a knack for finding danger, and for being in the wrong place at the right time. And as I got to know Ski, I found that this pattern of finding trouble was a continuation of his prewar life back home in the States.

On the streets of New Jersey, Ski blended into his rough urban landscape as just another kid on the corner. As a Polish immigrant in a tough neighborhood, he had a hard time navigating in his new homeland. He eventually ended up joining the Army National Guard to escape a downward cycle of problems at home and with the law. In time, he ended up in the heat of Afghanistan.

How it happened, or why, I don't know, but there in Afghanistan he was instantly, and seemingly effortlessly, transformed from the role of troublemaker into that of a noble American hero. Selfless. Compassionate. Brave.

But his kindness and good nature to those around him was only one side of the equation. Ski was lethal in combat, and he remains the bravest machine gunner I've ever seen in action. During the ambush when Ski was shot in the ear while manning the machine gun, he ducked down from the incoming fire just long enough to let me know he was hit, that he was pissed, and that he was going to get the guy who had shot him. Then he popped right back up in the turret to unleash a torrent of bullets and expletives.

No matter what the circumstances, Ski would choose the right path and do the right thing. Here, in the heat and dust of war, despite the mental and physical fatigue that cracked our minds and bodies, his moral compass was always pointing in the right direction. In Afghanistan, it never faltered when it mattered.

And then we came home. And for Ski, and for many like him, the transition to civilian life was perhaps harder than the war. The return to the civil and mundane life was like a withdrawal from a powerful drug. And in his case, this withdrawal brought out some demons, bad choices, and ultimately tragic consequences.

Although I hadn't seen Ski since we both got home from Afghanistan, I had been in regular phone and email contact with him, and I knew he had been having problems with reintegration. Fights, excessive drinking, and family strife were a daily occurrence. My life had also been rough going during this time, with my own batch of "transitional issues" (divorce, moving to a new house, and starting back at my busy civilian job). And with hundreds of miles between us, I was unable to be there for him like I wanted to be. Chaotic weeks passed before I was finally able to make the time to go see him in New Jersey.

Our reunion wasn't what I had hoped for. The loud, boisterous nature of our friendship was totally absent. This meeting was instead quiet and somber. I sat there with him, and told him in no uncertain terms that he needed to get his shit squared away. I reached into my social-worker bag of tricks, and mixed good, mature adult advice with salty infantry threats and obscenities. As a platoon leader and commander, it was a technique I had used many times on my wayward soldiers with good results.

But unfortunately my words were falling on deaf ears.

Ski, the vibrant, supercharged soldier, lay silently in a coma, oblivious to my pearls of wisdom, and for that matter, un-aware that I was even in his presence. Doctors said it was unlikely he would survive the head injuries he had suffered during his tragic foray to the wild side, and if he did it was unclear if he would remember me, the war, or anything of consequence. The only response to my profanity-laced lec-ture was the hum of medical equipment and the rhythmic pulse of a ventilator.

VANDY

Recently my friend Vandy came to visit me in New York for a weekend postwar reunion. Specialist Van De Walker, as he was formally known, had served as an ETT with me for the first half of my tour at FOB Ghazni, and was a regular out on missions with me and Ski. He was also an infantryman, assigned to the ANA *kandak's* heavy weapons company.

When I picked him up at the train station, I saw that his arms were covered in cuts and scabs. He was wearing a knee brace. His swollen and bruised knuckles suggested many punches thrown and landed. He told me all these injuries were the results of bar fights, some more successful than others.

From previous phone calls, I wasn't surprised to see these physical signs of a rough transition home. A few months ago, Vandy had called me excitedly after totaling his car in a drag race on a city street. I knew all this was not out of the ordinary for recently returned combat veterans.

Vandy's attitude at war was always "Damn the torpe-

Specialist Ryan Van De Walker, a.k.a. Vandy, riding in an ANA Ford Ranger pickup during pursuit of Taliban fighters in Andar, Ghazni Province.

does, full speed ahead." He had the closest life-and-death call of his tour just days before he left Afghanistan. This mission was one he didn't need to be on, but Vandy was the type who would volunteer to go. Most soldiers bunker down during their last days in country. I know I did. But Vandy wasn't one to play defense. He liked to run up the score.

As his convoy was returning to base, his Humvee was rocked by a suicide bomber. The blast came without warning, and he told me the destruction darkened the world like an eclipse of the sun, choking out the light with dust and smoke. Vandy continued to drive forward through the kill zone, as we are trained to do. As he exited the dust cloud, murky rays of sunlight peeked through the windows, obscured by the chunks of scorched dirt and sticky flesh that clung to the vehicle.

Vandy told me he wished he had been able to go back to treat the wounded civilians, even though that could have exposed him to a secondary explosion or ambush. Had he been in charge of the convoy, I have no doubt that's what he would have done. Not all the risks Vandy took were without merit.

During his visit, I coerced Vandy into accompanying me to my PTSD counseling appointment at our local vet center. He was hesitant, but we spent an awkward and difficult hour scratching the surface of his war-related issues with my counselor. Nothing miraculous happens in one counseling session, but maybe he took away something he can build on.

Vandy's visit was stressful for me. It was a reminder of what we had gone through in Afghanistan, and how it had changed us. And it reminded me of how close I have been to that edge of fights and car wrecks and bad decisions.

In a few months, Vandy will return to a combat zone with his National Guard unit. This time it will be Iraq. Knowing this made it all the harder to drop him off at the train station when it was time for him to return to Wisconsin. As we hugged good-bye, I couldn't help but smile. Vandy is tough, and despite his missteps, he still keeps moving forward. Full speed ahead.

OPERATION IRON RAGE REVISITED

Since I've been home, I've told and retold this story many times to friends, counselors, and family. The events, which I have described previously in the essay "Operation Iron Rage," still haunt me today. Allow me to retell the story and explain.

In that essay, I described a tragicomedy of my own errors that ended ultimately in accidental success. And I wrote that on a similar mountain, with a nearly identical mission that was much better planned and aggressively executed, my ETT buddy Deg died.

The two mountains where these two missions occurred lie in eastern Afghanistan. Sergeant First Class Bernard Deghand and I were given the same straightforward objectives: to assault a mountain, to destroy Taliban base camps, and ultimately, to kill or capture Taliban fighters. We were both ETTs. We had both conducted similar missions in the previous months in the same general area. But the similarities ended there.

My Afghan and American soldiers attacked a Taliban

camp we discovered on a mountain named Tand Ghar. The enemy was routed, and their base was destroyed by the artillery we requested. Word of this successful mission spread quickly through the international media pool that was covering the larger operation, and reporters desperate for a story were summarily embedded into my small group of ANA and ETTs. Within days, my merry band of warriors were heroes in my hometown press. I made it into the pages of newspapers across my home state, and my ugly mug was even on the nightly news in France.

And on the other side of the mountain range was my buddy Deg, who by all accounts did everything correctly and by the books on his mountain assault. Yet when his mission ended, he lay dead, through no fault of his own.

As I previously recounted, the details of my success are both comical and embarrassingly sophomoric. For the mission onto Tand Ghar, I had a couple of American soldiers and about fifty Afghans under my command. Despite high hopes for contact, a day had passed in our search without a single enemy encounter. The lack of action, coupled with the heat, had pushed us into a carefree and careless mind-set.

While having *chai* in yet another nameless village, we receive intel from the elders that the Taliban in fact had a night camp literally right next to us, on the top of Tand Ghar, a modest but impressive rocky mountain. We check it out with binos. We have A-10 fighters do a flyover. Nothing moves. Nothing is spotted. Our initial excitement wilts in the noonday sun.

Despite the lack of activity, I'm inclined to lead a climb up Tand Ghar. My fellow American soldiers are skeptical, and plead with me not to bother. Being the commander, I get the final say in the matter. But I issue a compromise order, and say only two squads of us will bother climbing to the top. The majority of Afghans and Americans will remain at the foot of the mountain.

By the time we make it three-quarters up the rocky slope, my group has shrunk from about twenty to only six Afghans, one fellow American, and an interpreter. Having succumbed to the groupthink of low expectations, I didn't even bother to bring a radio, or extra ammo, or to advise higher that we were embarking on this climb. I pretty much broke all the rules in the book, due to a complacency honed by months of wild-goose chases that turned up nothing. The other American and the interpreter, equally uninspired, had decided to shift to the right to get a better view of the valley for a couple of scenic photos, and were out of eyesight and earshot.

So it should be no surprise that I nearly dropped a deuce in my pants when all the Afghan soldiers, who were about forty meters ahead of me, began firing their AK-47s once they crested the ridge.

It was then that I fully realized the depth of my folly. I was on a wide-open rocky mountainside with nowhere to take cover, with no radio, and no interpreter, undermanned, and physically exhausted by the climb and the altitude. And to dramatically add a heaping dose of irony to this perilous situation, the Afghan soldiers whom I had left down at the base of the mountain mistook me for a Taliban and fired hundreds of medium and heavy machine-gun rounds at me as I moved along the ridgeline.

In the end, for reasons that remain unexplained and un- known, the larger, dug-in, and well-defended Taliban force on Tand Ghar decided to run. We routed them off the moun- tain and destroyed their camp with artillery. Despite my er- rors, we didn't suffer one friendly casualty.

And then there is my buddy Deg. He had many things going for him for his mission. His mountain assault was well planned, as he had days to prepare for it. He and his Afghan soldiers had even practiced the assault with American units that were also involved. He had a larger force of Afghans in the fight, more Americans on his left and right, and an interpreter literally by his side. He had radios, ammo, and everything that should have guaranteed success.

But it didn't. He was shot and killed by enemy small-arms fire as he moved up his mountain.

At this part of the story, I ask myself, "Why? Why did I live, and Deg die?"

A good story should have a proper ending, an explanation that puts everything in place and makes sense of the facts presented. A "moral of the story," if you will, seems necessary here given the severity of the outcome for Deg. Yet my story doesn't do any of these things. Instead it leaves the audience to consider such an unlikely outcome for both parties, and an equally frustrated, guilt-ridden, and confused storyteller.

In the end, I'm left with some pictures I took of Tand Ghar, some newspaper clippings of my "success," and a sense of remorse that maybe the wrong guy made it home alive.

PTSD: A BLOG AS THERAPY

It always happens the same way: A loud explosion catches me unsuspecting and unprepared. I feel my body violently flung skyward, propelled by a fierce blast wave.

And as quickly as this upward momentum has taken me, it lets go, and I'm free-falling back to earth. I see the ground getting closer and closer as I accelerate toward it.

I can feel the violent impact even before it occurs. My heart races, sometimes skips, as my body clenches for this inevitable collision with the ground.

But there is no impact.

Because there was no flight.

There was no flight, because there was no explosion.

Instead of a bomb or RPG going off, it's just a small noise that has caught me off guard, and triggers this reaction. Something as commonplace as a dropped soda can, a box thudding to the ground, thunder, a car door slamming shut, or a distant traffic noise. It doesn't matter what the source is, the result is always the same. I'm flying and falling, and it's terrifying.

It's post-traumatic stress disorder, better known as PTSD, the mind's inability to normally process and reconcile the daily experiences of life after prolonged exposure to combat. The terror, the fear, and the stress flood into the crevices of everyday experience. The slow-motion memories of bodies torn and bloodied fill one's mind at the most unlikely moments.

PTSD manifests itself in degrees of severity. Some soldiers can shrug off the trauma of combat, while others are completely paralyzed by it. I'm somewhere in the middle. Moments of calm, mixed with flashes of irrational fear. All provoked by the most mundane and seemingly innocent triggers.

I'm not ashamed to admit that I have been diagnosed with PTSD by Army medical officers. I, like many combat soldiers, am experiencing the problems of shaky nerves, anxiety, sleep loss, and appetite loss. We aren't crazy—we still laugh and joke and cry like any healthy human being. But PTSD is real, and it's difficult, and it's something that only time and open discussion with oneself, and with those close to us, can relieve.

I've explained to many people here that the experiences I've had in combat are like accruing an armful of heavy, jagged stones. During many missions, I am forced one by one to pick up and carry these metaphorical stones. This burden, if not lessened, is unbearable and cannot be sustained.

But I've found that writing these essays is an incredibly potent therapy. It's much more potent than any of the antidepressants and sleep medications being offered to me by the Army.

As irrational as it may seem, every one of you who reads these words and stories is in effect picking up one of the stones, and taking it away from me.

My living area, where most of these essays were written.

Knowing that real people, friends and strangers alike, are out there in a safe part of the world, sharing in these experiences, provides me with a sense of calm and release that is profound. It's like a small part of me is temporarily evacuated to your safe and calm corner of the world.

This may all sound melodramatic, but it's not. It's sincere. After each essay I write, the positive feedback and support comes rolling in. And when this happens, I feel like the experiences shared are no longer things I have to deal with alone. These weights are distributed, diluted, processed, and gone.

MY ALIVE DAY

One of the first things I did when I came home from Afghanistan on leave was tattoo the date 26 June 2006 on my right forearm. On this date, in a small village in Andar, I had my Alive Day. In the midst of an ambush by Taliban forces on our patrol, I heard the distinctive blast of an RPG being launched in front of me. I turned my head to see the football-shaped warhead searing through the air toward me.

It may sound like a cliché, but for the first time in my life time did slow down. Some part of my brain hit the slow-motion button and turned off the volume. The RPG landed in front of me. A ball of silent fire and dirt clumps filled my field of vision. I felt like I was watching it on TV with the volume turned off.

The eardrum-shattering explosion and the concussion were nonexistent. Don't get me wrong, they were there, but I didn't feel them or hear them. That's how I know this day was my Alive Day. Reality was suspended momentarily. The normal physical rules of life (sound, sensation) were paused, and in the process, my life was extended.

The ballast of the RPG that landed at my feet on my Alive Day, 26 June 2006. My Alive Day tattoo is partially visible on my arm.

Having an Alive Day has both good and bad effects. It has shown itself to be both a therapeutic tool and a danger-ous outlet. The downside is that I treat every day since my Alive Day as bonus time. It's easy to rationalize doing dumb or risky things because I'm playing with house money. I've heard many stories from my Afghan comrades—all with their own Alive Days—that involved an admission of en-gaging in high-risk behavior. Their stories all end with, "Yeah, it was dumb for me to do that, but I should be dead anyways, so what the fuck."

The positive side of the Alive Day is that whenever I am hosting a one-man pity party, I catch a glimpse of the date tattooed on my arm, and I remember that even a bad day being alive is better than a good day being dead.

BRONZE STARS FOR BROKEN SOULS

Two years have passed since the War Eagle and Black-foot ETT teams left Afghanistan. We came home to a supportive country and felt like heroes. Most of us were awarded Bronze Stars for our frequent combat engagements, along with a salad bowl of other minor medals and awards. Some of us have returned to normal lives, seemingly unchanged by our yearlong life as an ETT. But many of us still deal on a daily basis with the stresses, anxiety, and seemingly unquenchable quest for the adrenaline rush of combat.

My story is pretty common for a combat veteran. I went to war a married man of fifteen years, and a father of four. My wife and I had just purchased our dream house, which I referred to as our "forever house." I came home from the war and never once slept in this house. I bounced around from place to place, got legally separated, then divorced. I put my kids through a confusing and fast-paced emotional roller-coaster ride. Despite my attempts to explain my erratic and confusing actions, I don't think they could comprehend what PTSD was and how it had changed me. I drank too much, and fought a myriad of personal demons, all the while trying to help some of my ETT peers who were having an even harder time assimilating into civilian life.

But I was smart enough to get involved with counseling at the local vet center. Because of this timely counseling intervention, I was able to stay out of jail, out of the hospital, and a safe distance from the morgue, which is more than some of my ETT peers can say. Over time this counseling allowed me to rebuild my relationships with my job, my kids, and even start a new healthy marriage with my new wife.

Unfortunately, a few of my teammates were more reluctant to get counseling (or even admit they had problems), and some of them remain, even today, dysfunctional in employment, relationships, and general healthy living.

Being an ETT was both an honor and a curse. Living on the ANA FOBs, we were the ambassadors for the United States of America to the Afghan soldiers and civilians we interacted with every day. We wore the American flag on our shoulders with pride, and we knew every action we took would be the standard Afghans used to measure the honor, integrity, and trustworthiness of the United States. This was a measure I feel we met: ETTs were held in high esteem by our Afghan counterparts.

But being an ETT was also a curse. We were asked by our higher-ups to do more with less, and we were shouldered with the expectation of transforming the primordial soup that is the ANA into a disciplined and organized fighting force. Any progress we may have made in this area was small and hard to measure, but progress was made.

We were asked to assume risks that no traditional American Army unit would submit their soldiers to. We did not have a security bubble between us and the Afghans.

ETTs were constantly surrounded by armed Afghan men, be they soldiers in the ANA or village elders in unfriendly remote towns. We did not have the sense of security that is commonly found among soldiers who fight and patrol alongside their friends and peers in traditional Army units. This is not to say Afghan soldiers were not our friends—they were, and many have laid down their lives to protect their ETTs. But in a life-and-death situation, there is a huge difference between being in combat with one lone American soldier, versus being in harm's way with a platoon of U.S. soldiers, with high-tech commo, weapons, medical skills, and evacuation assets. Americans speak the same language, and are sworn to a code of never leaving a fallen comrade behind. This was the extra degree of difficulty that the ETTs faced whenever we went outside the wire.

An unexpected reunion with Ski, a few weeks after he awoke from his coma.

War is a crapshoot for everyone who is in harm's way, and many different types of American soldiers could compare their jobs to that of an ETT, and make similar claims about the levels of danger they faced. We as ETTs did not hold any monopoly on hardship in Afghanistan, and we are no more heroes than our fellow American soldiers in traditional Army units. But for the ETTs I worked with, there is no questioning that we had to embrace the suck in ways that regular soldiers never did, and that we earned our rightful place at the tip of the counterinsurgency spear.

THE END

This is my final essay. Soon this blog will vanish from the Internet. Before it goes, I wanted to thank the thousands of readers who have followed along on this yearlong ramble with me through Afghanistan. But now, I feel it's time to pen the final chapter on my story.

Chronicling this Afghan adventure through this blog has been the most therapeutic and powerful medication to help fight the depression, sadness, and anxiety I've experienced here. It also has been a way to share the experiences of my brave teammates, and the humor and chaos that filled our days.

Through this blog, I've made many new friends, real and virtual. This blog served as a tool that collected winter clothing for hundreds of Afghan children, and some of the writings morphed into radio commentaries heard by tens of thousands of people across the globe. The net result was a sharing of experiences that strengthened people's connection to the war, the soldiers, and the Afghan people.

Ultimately, mine was just one of many voices in this

wilderness, and this voice is no longer needed. Some will fill the space with their own perspectives and experiences. Some will prove to be far greater storytellers than I could ever hope to be. So I move out of the line, and hope that the tragic and heroic and weathered story of this war will continue to move forward, and that no one will forget what is happening in Afghanistan.

EPILOGUE

BIG BROTHER IS WATCHING,
AND HE SEEMS TO BE ENJOYING IT

Was there censorship in Afghanistan? Did any of my writings get edited by higher-level commanders? Was what you have read my truthful opinion, or was I implanting themes and messages to promote propagandistic agendas being pushed by public affairs staff at higher levels of command? In an era of documented manipulation of the media by various entities within the Department of Defense, the answer may surprise you.

Over 90 percent of these essays were written as blogs and posted online. A small number of them were then recorded and broadcast for various regional and national media outlets. All of this occurred while I was on orders, on active duty, and subject to a myriad of confusing rules and regulations pertaining to uniformed members of the military having direct and public media exposure via the Internet. Never once was anything I wrote censored by higher levels of command. This wasn't because they all shared an enlightened concern for freedom of speech. To the contrary, there were times they wanted to stop me from writing.

Their failure to censor was more a result of my remote position as an ETT, and the nebulous and evolving rules governing blogs and direct contact with the media at that time. This ultimately gave me a lot of maneuver space to write and speak bluntly and honestly without any effectual interference from higher levels of command.

If an ETT on a small, isolated FOB asked permission to publish or speak, and then waited for the proper authorizations up and down the chain before doing so, very little would ever make it into the public sphere. At all levels of Task Force Phoenix, to which all ETTs belonged, communication was slow and disjointed from battalion to brigade to corps and eventually up to Camp Phoenix. Given this fact, my approach from day one was to ignore my chain of command, submit the works directly for public consumption, and then cross my fingers and hope the quality of my work would shield me from flak. It was a risky strategy, but many fellow writers in Afghanistan were doing the same thing without too much blowback. I had learned years ago that in the Army, it's better to ask forgiveness than it is to ask permission.

The first time I got wind of higher-ups monitoring my writing was when word came to me from a sympathetic contact in the Task Force Phoenix public affairs section that our commanding general had personally read some of my postings. In fact, this contact told me that the general had used portions of one of my essays in his stump speech during travels in the Middle East and back in the United States. Instead of a reprimand or a muzzle, I got praise for telling compelling, honest, true stories of the important work we ETTs were doing in a positive and credible manner. The public affairs section, with a wink and a nod, said, "Keep it up."

At the same time, lower levels of my command also

became aware of my writings. I received a moderately hostile email from my brigade commander demanding that any future essays I wrote would have to be submitted for approval through my chain of command. I responded, "Roger that, sir!" but continued to write and publish without allowing this order to impede my actions. I knew that the intent of this requirement was effectively to shut me down, and I didn't want to accept barricades between me and the public. If push came to shove, and these midlevel commanders wanted to bust me, I had the commanding general as my ace in the hole to pull my nuts out of the fire. My writings were honest and supportive of the mission, did not jeopardize operational security in any way, and were having a real impact on people at home who had all but forgotten about the war in Afghanistan.

This approach worked well, and for many months I never received one reprimand or punishment for my continued writing and speaking. Either my midlevel commanders lost interest in me or they recognized my writings had merit, and that I was held in high esteem by their boss, the general, and so they never cracked down on me.

This pattern of me publishing unfettered continued until the "heart problem" in the winter of 2007. The essay "Pieces in the Snow," which I recorded for National Public Radio from my bunker-like hooch in Sharana, blew apart this media truce much like the suicide bomber in the essay blew himself apart.

Because I was on a remote FOB, most if not all contact with higher came via email. And so it was that the highest level of command in country, CSTC-A, had sent a nasty email to Task Force Phoenix demanding that I be silenced and punished for going public with this essay. The rationale was that it was too violent, and the message that it sent contradicted the themes of "construction" and "rebuilding" as the focus of our presence in Afghanistan. Images of violence and brutality were not desirable for public consumption back home, and my description of the ANA soldier kicking the suicide bomber's heart down the road like a soccer ball was too much for CSTC-A to handle.

CSTC-A was the boss of Task Force Phoenix, which meant their two-star general trumped my one-star general, and I expected to have some negative ramifications for my actions. Fortunately, I wasn't the only rogue media element in theater, and my friends in the Phoenix public affairs section hoodwinked CSTC-A by giving them the impression that I was being properly counseled and punished, all the while sending me emails of praise for the work I was doing. It was a bold move on their part, and an example of how they "got it" when it came to public opinion back home. Task Force Phoenix, the command for all ETTs, was well aware of how difficult the war was, and of the future sacrifices that would be needed to ensure a victory in Afghanistan. I would argue, maybe unfairly, that the people at the CSTC-A public affairs shop, living on Bagram, were sufficiently removed from this reality, and only wanted to portray a rosy view of how things were progressing in Afghanistan. If the truth didn't fit the warm fuzzy "message of the day," it didn't see the light of day.

It was never my intent to be a propagandist or spokesperson for or against the war in Afghanistan. As a progressive-minded person, I have always been skeptical of the simplistic justifications for war, and the saccharine feel of good stories that hide the true costs of combat. Ironically, some readers and listeners to my stories accused me of just this. I can honestly say that I never intentionally infused my writings with any of my criticisms of America's excessive use of military force abroad, nor did I ever try to sugarcoat things that we were doing well. The truth for me was that the war in Afghanistan is a conundrum of positive, humanistic goals bloodied by the violence used to combat those who resist them.

In conclusion, it's fair to say that what I wrote never pleased everyone, but it was honest and fair enough, with enough supporters planted in the various levels of command, that it went uncensored for the whole year I lived and fought in Afghanistan.